Pursuing Righteousness

Sandra Roberts

Zameiru Ministries

Pursuing Righteousness

Pursuing Righteousness

Copyright @2024 by Sandra Roberts

Print ISBN: 978-0-473-72385-9

Unless otherwise stated, all Bible quotations are taken from the NEW KING JAMES VERSION (NKJV): Scripture taken from the NEW KING JAMES VERSION®. Copyright© 1982 by Thomas Nelson, Inc. Used by permission. All rights reserved.

Scriptures marked NLT are taken from the HOLY BIBLE, NEW LIVING TRANSLATION (NLT): Scriptures taken from the HOLY BIBLE, NEW LIVING TRANSLATION, Copyright© 1996, 2004, 2007 by Tyndale House Foundation. Used by permission of Tyndale House Publishers, Inc., Carol Stream, Illinois 60188. All rights reserved. Used by permission.

All rights reserved under International Copyright Law. Contents and Cover may not be reproduced in whole or in part without the written permission of the author.

Cover Design by Ratnam Renu.

Cover Image by Fulvio Ambrosanio.

Wheat photo by Sandra Roberts.

Edited by Richard Roberts.

Additional editorial services by Dominion Unlimited Publications.

All rights reserved.

No portion of this book can be translated or reproduced in any form, without the written permission of the publisher or author, Sandra Roberts, except as permitted by U.S. copyright law.

Published by Zameiru Ministries

zameiru.ministries@gmail.com

Foreword

For the last three years God has been teaching me much about the Kingdom of God. There is still much to learn.

It has been on my heart to "pursue righteousness," which is where the title of this book comes from (Matthew 6:33).

I believe the fivefold ministry listed in Ephesians 4:11-18 are to equip, train, build up the body to bring it to unity and knowledge of the Son of God, to bring the body to perfection (maturity) so everyone can fulfil God's plan and destiny for their life. This means that each believer grows into a fully mature son (Huios).

There should be no schism or division in the body (1 Corinthians 12:25-27), and everyone should do their part. The foot cannot be a hand, nor the eye be an ear. Not all members are visible, but all have a very important part.

Foreword

We have been given a mission to take the Gospel to the ends of the earth. We preach the Kingdom, with signs and wonders following the preaching of the Word, to see lives redeemed from darkness and the demonic, and transferred into God's Kingdom, the Kingdom of light. We have been made His ambassadors to take His precious Word to the ends of the earth, that His Father's house might be full. Amen.

Then His Kingdom will be manifested on earth and the Gospel will go to the ends of the earth so the Lord can return in all His glory, with the angels. The dead in Christ will rise first, then we who are alive will be caught up with Him and the angels at the trumpet sound (1 Thessalonians 4:16-17). This is the hope for every believer and makes us different from every other religion.

Contents

1. INTRODUCTION	9
So, who is Melchizedek?	15
2. WHAT IS RIGHTEOUSNESS?	17
3. THE KINGDOM OF GOD	25
The Message of the Kingdom	27
4. KEYS OF THE KINGDOM	35
The First Key: Praise and Worship.	35
Secondly, You Need to Know the Key of Authority.	38
The Third Key is The Anointing.	39
The Fourth Key is Prayer with Fasting	41
5. UNDERSTANDING THE KINGDOM THROUGH JESUS' PARABLES	45
Section One - The Parables of the Seed and of Harvest	47
The Parable of the Wheat and the Tares (Matthew 13:24-30; 36-43)	51
The Parable of the Mustard Seed (Matthew 13:31)	58
Section Two – Parables of Prayer/Persistence and Judgement	62
Section Three – Parables of the Wedding Feasts	85
Section Four - Parables on Faithfulness and Stewardship	90
Section Five - Parables of Mercy and the Love of God	105

6. CHARACTER (CULTURE) OF THE
   KINGDOM   123
7. MYSTERIES OF THE KINGDOM   155
   The Four Levels of Reading In Hebraic
   Thinking   157
   The Mystery of His Will   161
   The Mystery of the Gospel/Salvation   165
   Inclusion of the Gentiles in the Plan of
   Salvation   167
   The Mystery of His Fellowship   170
   The Mystery is of the Relationship of a
   Man and a Woman   171

   Conclusion   175
   About the Author   177

Chapter 1
Introduction

WE ARE TOLD IN MATTHEW 6:33 TO *"SEEK FIRST THE kingdom of God **and His righteousness** and all these things shall be added unto you (us)."*

Therefore, getting righteousness must be pretty important. As we grow in knowledge of the Kingdom of God, we will need to study this aspect more and more as it is pivotal to knowledge of the Kingdom and how it functions.

We know that a kingdom must have a King, as it is the domain of the king over which he rules and reigns. Jesus is the King of kings and Lord of lords over His Kingdom. However, He we will reign with Him when we become a **mature Son** (the Greek word is *huios)*. We are co-labourers with Him.

*"For the Kingdom of God is not eating and drinking, but **righteousness**, peace and joy in the Holy Spirit." (Romans 4:17)*

We are told in 2 Timothy 2:22 to *"Flee also youthful lusts; **but pursue (chase after) righteousness**, faith, love and peace with those who call on the Lord out of a pure heart."*

There are many verses in Proverbs we will look at in this little book, but for now let's look at Proverbs 15:9:

"He who loves Him (the Lord) follows righteousness."

Another version says He, (the Lord) loves those who **pursue righteousness.** [This is where I have taken the title of this book from.] Is this you? I don't know about you, but I want to be loved by the Lord. Therefore, I choose to pursue righteousness.

"To do righteousness and justice is more acceptable to the Lord than sacrifice." (Proverbs 21:3)

Then in verse 21, *"He who **follows righteousness and mercy (kindness),** finds life, righteousness and honour."* Do you realise the importance of mercy and kindness? It goes hand in hand with righteousness.

Some Jewish scholars say there are 613 commandments of God in the Old Covenant, which is summed up in the 10 commandments. But then there is the Scripture in Micah 6:8, which others say sums up the Old Testament.

> *"He has shown you, O man, what is good; and what does the Lord REQUIRE of you, but to do justly (walk in justice), show mercy (kindness). And to walk humbly with your God."*

So, to walk in justice, mercy and humility are very important character qualities. This is because they are qualities of God Himself. We know the more we spend time with Him, the more we become like Him and reflect Him.

> *"But we all with unveiled face, beholding as in a mirror the glory of the Lord, are being transformed into the same image from glory to glory, just as by the Spirit of the Lord." (2Corinthians 3:18)*

This simply means as we behold His righteousness, we become more righteous. As we behold His justice, we become more just. As we behold His lovingkindness, we become more loving. As we behold His mercy, we become more merciful to others as Jesus laid out in the Sermon on the Mount. He also added in Matthew 5:6:

*"Blessed are those who **hunger and thirst for righteousness,** for they shall be filled (satisfied)."*

Clearly, we need to not only pursue righteousness, but also hunger and thirst for it.

We know God made man and woman in the beginning of creation. He blessed them and told them to be fruitful and multiply. He told them to subdue the fish, birds and animals and have dominion (rulership) over all creation. Mankind was made to rule and reign in the earth. When Adam sinned, he lost the glory with which he was clothed. The Hebrew word for glory is weight. The weight of His glory. This is what mankind lost because of sin. They lost the ability to rule and reign in life. But through Christ we are co-labourers and will rule and reign with Him.

"For we are both God's workers. And you are God's field. You are God's building." (1Corinthians 3:9)

We will rule and reign with Christ as fully mature sons *(huios).*

Do you know God was not caught by surprise when Adam and Eve fell? He had already made provision for forgiveness through the Cross and through His Son coming to earth as the perfect Lamb of God. Did you know He was slain before the foundation of the world?

For God loved the world so much He sent His only son to come and die for the sins of the world, that we might be forgiven and reconciled back to God and made righteous before Him.

> *"All who dwell on the earth will worship Him, whose names have not been written in the **Book of Life of the Lamb slain before the foundation of the world.**" (Revelation 13:8)*

> *"But with the precious blood of Christ, as of a lamb without blemish and without spot. He indeed was **foreordained before the foundation of the world**, but was manifest in these last times for you, who through Him believe in God, who raised Him from the dead and gave Him glory, so that your faith and hope are in God." (1Peter 1:19-21)*

There is a beautiful picture of the Cross in Psalm 85:10-11. It says *"Mercy and truth have met together; Righteousness and peace have kissed. Truth shall spring out of the earth, and **Righteousness** shall look down from heaven."*

Simply, righteousness is at the top (from Heaven) with truth at the bottom (springing out of the earth), while mercy and truth meet (kiss) in the middle! (This is where the book cover comes from!)

Psalm 37:5-6 tells us when we commit our way to the Lord and trust in Him, *"He shall bring forth your **righteousness** as the light and your justice as the noonday."* Verse 21 tells us, *"The **righteous** shows mercy and gives."* Then in verse 25 it says, *"Yet I have never seen the **righteous** begging bread,"* and verse 30, *"The mouth of the **righteous** speaks wisdom and his tongue talks of justice; The law of God is in his heart; None of his steps shall slide."* Again verse 39 says *"But the salvation of the **righteous** is from the Lord; He is their strength in time of trouble; And the Lord shall help them and deliver them; He shall deliver them from the wicked, and save them, because they trust in Him."*

Here we have some amazing promises from God: of light and justice, provision, wisdom, knowledge of the law of God, not to slide or stumble, strength in our time of need, and deliverance from the wicked when we walk with Him and trust in Him. Many people trust in their own way, but we know most ways lead to death. The way of God leads to life.

> *"There is a path before each person that seems right, but it ends in death." (Proverbs 14:12)*

One of the names of Christ is Melchizedek. (*Melech* = king, *tszidek* = **righteous**, so **King of righteousness.**) We know when Jesus died the temple curtain was rent in two, from top to bottom. God supernaturally made the way open for not only the High priest to enter, but all Israelites and even us, as Gentiles (Matthew 27:51).

"So also, Christ did not glorify Himself to become High Priest, but it was He who said to Him: 'You are My Son, today I have begotten you.' As He also says in another place, 'You are a priest forever, according to the order of Melchizedek.'"

"He suffered and was perfected through His obedience, to become the author of eternal salvation to all who obey Him, called by God as High priest according to the order of Melchizedek." (Hebrews 5:5-10)

So, who is Melchizedek?

He is a type of Christ, first mentioned in the book of Genesis 14:18-20, as the **king of Righteousness** and King of Salem (JeruSALEM peace). He suddenly appeared to Abraham to whom He gave bread and wine and a blessing in the name of El Elyon (God Most High). So, he was also a priest of the Most High God. Abraham, in return gave him a tenth of all he had.

The Jewish sages believe he was Shem, the son of Noah who went East. He is also mentioned in Psalm 110:4, a Messianic psalm, saying *'You are a priest forever according to the order of Melchizedek'.* You can also read in Matthew 22: 41:45, *That the Christ is the Son of David. So how does David call Him Lord saying, "The Lord said to my Lord, sit at MY right hand, Til I make your enemies your footstool."*

Notice Melchizedek gave Abraham bread and wine. This resembles the Lord's supper that we celebrate as communion. In the Old Testament, you could not be a king and a priest, but in the New Testament, He has made us **both kings** (of the kingly line) **and priests** (who offer worship to God).

> *"and has made us kings and priests to His God and Father, to Him be glory and dominion forever and ever. Amen."* (Revelation 1:6)

This is our spiritual inheritance—to become mature sons of God and reflect His glory in the earth and to worship Him as the 'Name above all names'.

Chapter 2
What is Righteousness?

THE WORD **RIGHTEOUS** MEANS UPRIGHT, IN RIGHT relationship with God, having your sins forgiven – being free from the guilt of sin. Of course, we know that God is righteous. He is the "judge of all the earth and will do RIGHT" (Genesis 18:25). As we become like HIM, we will mirror His **righteousness.**

In the Old Testament, they were made righteous by their faith.

> *"By faith Abel offered to God a more excellent sacrifice than Cain, through which he obtained witness that he was **righteous**, God testifying of his gifts; and through it he being dead still speaks."* **(Hebrews 11:4)**

*"By faith Noah, being divinely warned of things not yet seen, moved with godly fear, prepared an ark for the saving of his household, by which he condemned the world and became **heir of the righteousness** which is according to faith."* (Hebrews 11:7)

*"And he (Abraham), believed in the Lord, and He accounted it to him for **righteousness.**"* **(Genesis 15:6 (see also Romans 4:3; Galatians 3:6))**

*"And the Scripture was fulfilled which says, "Abraham believed God, and it was accounted to him **for righteousness**." And he was called the <u>friend of God</u>." (*James 2:23)

We know when we put our faith and trust in Jesus Christ that we are made righteous and justified (just as if there was no sin). See Romans 3:21-26 below.

"But now the righteousness of God apart from the law is revealed, being witnessed by the Law and the Prophets, even the righteousness of God, through faith in Jesus Christ, to all and on all who believe. For there is no difference; for all have sinned and fall short of the glory of God, being justified freely by His grace through the redemption that is in Christ Jesus, whom God

> *set forth as a propitiation by His blood, through faith, to demonstrate His righteousness, because in His forbearance God had passed over the sins that were previously committed, to demonstrate at the present time His righteousness, that He might be just and the justifier of the one who has faith in Jesus." (Romans 3:21-26)*

In other words, all whom believe in Jesus Christ through faith, have received grace (unmerited favour) to be justified (made right with God), and redeemed (bought with a price). The wrath of God against our sin and everything evil in the earth is called 'propitiation' – betrayal, false witnesses, scamming, theft, murder, rape, kidnapping, sex trafficking, abuse, bombing—whatever you can name—has been satisfied by Jesus' pure blood sacrificed for us.

> *"and, this is love, not that we loved God, but that He loved us and sent His Son to be the propitiation for our sins." (1John 4:10)*

That is what propitiation means. He has 'passed over' our sin (blotted it out) so it remains no more and we are righteous before Him. When Jesus died, the veil was torn in two, so we have access to the mercy seat in the Holy of Holies. Therefore, we can come boldly before the throne of God with no guilt or condemnation because He has made us righteous. Halleluyah!

There is much about this also in Romans chapter 5:

> *"Therefore, having been justified by faith, we have peace with God through our Lord Jesus Christ,... For when we were still without strength, in due time Christ died for the ungodly. For scarcely for a righteous man will one die; yet perhaps for a good man someone would even dare to die. But God demonstrates His own love toward us, in that <u>while we were still sinners, Christ died for us.</u> Much more then, having now been justified by His blood, we shall be saved from wrath through Him. For if when we were enemies we were reconciled to God through the death of His Son, much more, having been reconciled, we shall be saved by His life. And not only that, but we also rejoice in God through our Lord Jesus Christ, through whom we have now received the reconciliation." (Romans 5:1, 6-11)*

Through the death of Christ, we are now made right with God through His shed blood. We are no longer His enemies but have been reconciled through His life laid down for us. Therefore, we can rejoice having right standing with God.

> *"For if by the one man's offense many died (Adam), much more the grace of God and the gift by the grace of the one Man, Jesus Christ,*

*abounded to many. And the gift is not like that which came through the one who sinned. For the judgment which came from one offense resulted in condemnation, but the free gift which came from many offenses resulted in justification. For if by the one man's offense death reigned through the one, much more those who receive abundance of grace and of the **gift of righteousness** will reign in life through the One, Jesus Christ."* (v12-17)

The sin of Adam brought death, curse and separation from God, but God's grace in Christ brought life and justification and the gift of righteousness.

*"Therefore, as through one man's offense judgment came to all men, resulting in condemnation, even so through one man's **righteous** act the free gift came to all men, resulting in justification of life. For as by one man's disobedience many were made sinners (Adam), so also by one Man's obedience many will be made **righteous** (Christ)." (Romans 5:18-19)*

Adam, who brought death on mankind by his disobedience, is contrasted with Christ, who through His obedience made us righteous. Adam is called the first Adam, but Christ is called the second Adam.

> *"Moreover, the law entered that the offense might abound. But where sin abounded, grace abounded much more, so that as sin reigned in death, even so grace might reign through righteousness to eternal life through Jesus Christ our Lord."* (Romans 5:20-21)

God shows us (whoever puts their faith in Jesus Christ) and demonstrates His righteousness by forgiving and justifying us. This proves His love for us, and He justified us while still being in sin, by His holy blood shed for us. Then we are reconciled (made in right relationship with God) so we can stand before Him. This is the miracle of the Cross.

> *"For, to this you were called, because Christ also suffered for us, leaving us an example, that you should follow His steps: "Who committed no sin, Nor deceit found in His mouth"; who, when He was reviled, did not revile in return; when He suffered, He did not threaten, but committed Himself to Him who judges righteously; who Himself bore our sins in His own body on the tree, that we, having died to sins, <u>might live for righteousness</u>—by whose stripes you were healed."* (1Peter 2:21-24)

Through Adam (the first man), sin and offense came into the world. This separated us from God and led to spiritual death and judgement. However, because of the sacrifice of Jesus Christ (the second Adam), grace came to mankind, through faith, to be forgiven and justified and reconciled. It is the free gift of God that allows us to be righteous and reign in life through Jesus Christ. By His righteous act, the free gift came to all men who believe, resulting in justification of life, and righteousness to eternal life through Jesus Christ our Lord. He willingly gave up His life for us (as a lamb led to the slaughter, without fighting or reviling) taking our place as sin (whatever you can name), spiritual death, curse and even sickness so we can be set free from all of that.

There is NO SUCH THING as our own righteousness. The prophet Isaiah said *"our righteousness is as filthy rags in His sight"* [rather disgusting] (Isaiah 64:6). Some people try and EARN THEIR SALVATION by doing good works. (Some religions even go door to door to try and 'earn their salvation'.) But we have already seen it is the <u>free gift of God</u> to all who believe, and it is only by His grace, and through faith in Him that we can be saved.

Our Good Deeds and Faith Explained

Good deeds are NEVER about salvation, but should FOLLOW our salvation. However, so you are not confused, the book of James talks about **'our good deeds"** and how 'faith without works is dead" (James

2:24,26). Let me explain. In verse 18, James said *"I will show you my faith BY MY WORKS."* You have to understand that <u>faith in Christ came first</u> and the works were a manifestation of his faith.

> *"Pure and undefiled religion before God and the Father is this: to visit orphans and widows in their trouble, and to keep oneself unspotted from the world."* (James 1:27)

We read in Psalm 37:21, *"The righteous shows mercy and gives."* This giving to the poor is part of the heart of God. There was a time in my life when I had little compassion for the poor and needy, but through reading the Scriptures and starting to understand what was on the heart of God, it also became something on my heart.

By His grace, through faith, I have been able to help establish now, two schools in Pakistan, help feed widows and orphans, the elderly, help flood and famine-stricken people in Pakistan and East Africa and help orphans go to school – revelation a long time after my salvation!

Chapter 3
The Kingdom of God

The Kingdom of God is like a multifaceted diamond. There are many different aspects to it. We cannot cover every aspect in this small book, but we will look at some of the most important ones.

We know that a kingdom must have a King, as it is the domain of the king over which he rules and reigns. Jesus is the King of kings and Lord of lords over His Kingdom. However, He allows us to reign with Him when we become a mature Son.

Jesus taught us to pray: *"Let your kingdom come, let your will be done on earth as it is in heaven"* (Matthew 6:10)!

Whenever we show the love of God in our actions, pray for someone, heal or deliver them in Jesus Christ's name, then the kingdom of God comes to earth.

There are two kingdoms. The kingdom of God or light and the kingdom of the Devil or darkness. But when we believe in Christ, we are *"delivered (translated, transferred) from the kingdom of darkness and conveyed (transferred) into the kingdom of the Son of His Love in whom we have redemption through His blood, the forgiveness of sins"* (Colossians 1:13-14).

Because we no longer live in the kingdom of darkness, we no longer live in the previous ways of darkness, as we are made *"new creatures in Christ. The old has gone and the new has come"* (2 Corinthians 5:17). Now it is time to learn to 'live by the spirit' and so glorify God in all that we do. Amen.

To enter the Kingdom, we have to be "born again." There is a natural birth (of water) and a spiritual birth (by God's Spirit).

> *"Jesus answered and said to him, 'Most assuredly, I say to you, unless one is born again, he cannot see the kingdom of God.'" (John 3:3)*

> *"Jesus answered, 'Most assuredly, I say to you, unless one is born of water and the Spirit, he cannot enter the kingdom of God. That which is born of the flesh is flesh, and that which is born of the Spirit is spirit'." (John 3:5-6)*

The Message of the Kingdom

When Jesus announced His Kingdom on earth He said *"The time is fulfilled and the Kingdom of God is at hand (ready). Repent and believe"* (Mark 1:15). Just two things needed. Repentance is a turning from our rebellion and our own ways and surrendering to His ways (the ways of the King and His Kingdom). It involves a change of thinking. Our beliefs must now line up with the Word of God and what He says about us. We are 'no longer under the curse, but under blessing', destined to be the 'head and not the tail'.

Many people have a slave mindset. You have to do what you are told because you are under the law of sin and death. However, in Christ, we are new creations, set free from the curse of the law of sin and death, and brought into the blessing of Abraham (Galatians 3:13-14). This means we don't have to try and earn our salvation by 'being good'. This is a religious action, but not true Christianity (relationship-based).

It also means where maybe there was bitterness and unforgiveness, we now learn to forgive. Where there was hatred, we learn to love. Where there was anger, jealousy, competition and envy we take these things off and replace them with love and kindness as these negative things do not belong in the Kingdom of God. They are part of the darkness we have come out of.

The second thing is believing in the Gospel. This firstly means believing in Jesus Christ, who is the Messiah. *Jesus* means salvation, *Yeshua* in Hebrew. *Christ* means the *'anointed one'*. This is the one who 'preached the Gospel to the poor, healed the broken-hearted, brought the prisoners out of the prisons (includes spiritual prisons of addiction and ungodly sin patterns), set the captives free from every sin and yoke of bondage and demonic power/oppression/possession, and preached the acceptable year of the Lord (day of salvation).

When Jesus read from the scroll of Isaiah 61 in Luke 4, after His baptism and wilderness experience of overcoming the Devil, He announced He was the Messiah with these same words, except He added, 'opens the eyes of the blind'.

> *"The Spirit of the LORD is upon Me, Because He has anointed Me To preach the gospel to the poor; He has sent Me to heal the broken hearted, To proclaim liberty to the captives And recovery of sight to the blind, To set at liberty those who are oppressed; To proclaim the acceptable year of the LORD."* (Luke 4:18-19)

> *"And Jesus went about all Galilee, teaching in their synagogues, preaching the gospel of the kingdom, and healing all kinds of sickness and all kinds of disease among the people. Then His fame*

> *went throughout all Syria; and they brought to Him all sick people who were afflicted with various diseases and torments, and those who were demon-possessed, epileptics, and paralytics; and He healed them. Great multitudes followed Him—from Galilee, and from Decapolis, Jerusalem, Judea, and beyond the Jordan."*
> (Matthew 4:23-35)

Here we see He preached the Gospel of the Kingdom, and as a result, ALL kinds of sickness and infirmity were healed as well as the demon-possessed being set free. If you do not know the geography of Israel, Galilee is in the north, Decapolis, in the middle, while Judea and Jerusalem are in the South. Syria is northeast, and the areas beyond the Jordan are further southeast. So, His fame went throughout a huge territory.

> *"When evening had come, they brought to Him many who were demon-possessed. And He cast out the spirits with a word, and healed all who were sick, that it might be fulfilled which was spoken by Isaiah the prophet, saying: 'He Himself took our infirmities and bore our sicknesses.'"*
> (Matthew 8:16-17)

Again, we see Jesus healing and delivering a huge multitude. He makes reference to Isaiah 53, where Jesus carried our sorrows (griefs) and bore our sickness:

"Surely, He has borne our griefs (traumas) And carried our sorrows (sicknesses, struggles, pains, difficulties); Yet we esteemed Him stricken, Smitten by God, and afflicted. But He was wounded for our transgressions (sins and iniquities), He was bruised for our iniquities (selfishness and rebellion); The chastisement for our peace (well-being) was upon Him, And by His stripes we are healed (made whole)." (Isaiah 53:4-5)

Jesus was whipped 39 times with a whip that contained pieces of metal that tore at His flesh, making His back *"like a ploughed field"* (Psalm129:3). He suffered what the Bible calls scourging, so that we could be healed by His stripes—one stripe for cancer, one for diabetes, one for arthritis, one for fever, one for heart problems, one for women's problems, one for every pain and infirmity you can name, including mental problems. Doctors say there are 39 different types or groups of sickness and disease.

There came a time in the life of John the Baptist when he had some doubts, so he sent messengers to Jesus to ask if He was the Messiah, or should they look for someone else?

"Jesus told them, 'Go back to John and tell him what you have heard and seen - the blind see, the lame walk, those with leprosy are cured, the deaf

hear, the dead are raised to life, and the Good News is being preached to the poor.' And he added, 'God blesses those who do not fall away because of me." (Matthew 11:4-6)

Just before Jesus ascended to the Father, He spoke these words – obviously very important as they were His <u>"Last words on earth!"</u>

"And then He told them, 'Go into all the world and preach the Good News to everyone. Anyone who believes and is baptized will be saved. But anyone who refuses to believe will be condemned. ***These miraculous signs will accompany those who believe: They will cast out demons in my name, and they will speak in new languages. They will be able to handle snakes with safety, and if they drink anything poisonous, it won't hurt them. They will be able to place their hands on the sick, and they will be healed.'"*** (Mark 16:15-18)

So, we have been given a commission to do the works that He did. In fact, Jesus said we would do greater things than He did (John 14:2)!

"Most assuredly, I say to you, he who believes in Me, the works that I do he will do also; and

*greater works than these he will do, because I go to My Father." (*John 14:12)

Further we see in Luke 9, Jesus gave power and authority to the twelve disciples and sent them to preach the Gospel of the Kingdom and heal the sick.

> *"Then He called His twelve disciples together and gave them power and authority over all demons, and to cure diseases. He sent them to preach the kingdom of God and to heal the sick."* (Luke 9:1-2)
>
> *After these things the Lord appointed seventy others also, and sent them two by two before His face into every city and place where He Himself was about to go."* (Luke 10:1)
>
> *"And heal the sick there, and say to them, 'The kingdom of God has come near to you.'"* (verse 9)

So, in Luke 10, He send out the 70 disciples. We know He gave them the same authority and power over sickness (verse 9) and over demons as they said the demons were subject to them (verse 17).

> *"Then the seventy returned with joy, saying, 'Lord, even the demons are subject to us in Your name.'"* (verse 17)

Then we see in verse 19, Jesus gave authority over ALL the works of the Devil, with a promise that nothing would hurt us!

"Behold, I give you the authority to trample on serpents and scorpions, and over all the power of the enemy, and nothing shall by any means hurt you." (Luke 10:19)

Paul, the Apostle, talked about <u>signs and wonders following the preaching of the Word</u> wherever he went:

"They were convinced by the power of miraculous signs and wonders and by the power of God's Spirit. In this way, I have fully presented the Good News of Christ from Jerusalem all the way to Illyricum." (Romans 15:19)

"And my message and my preaching were very plain. Rather than using clever and persuasive speeches, I relied only on the power of the Holy Spirit." (1Corinthians 2:4)

As Paul relied on the Holy Spirit and spoke the word of God plainly, people were saved, healed and set free, and signs and wonders followed his preaching. This is the message of the Kingdom—to preach the Good News of salvation (that's what the word Gospel means), followed by demonstration of His mighty power to heal the sick, cast out the demons, to bring hope and peace, to heal the broken-hearted and traumatised, etc.

Personally, I believe if there are no signs and wonders following your preaching, you need to ask yourself, "What kind of Gospel are you preaching?"

Chapter 4
Keys of the Kingdom

"I give you keys of the kingdom of heaven…"

— Matthew 16

WISDOM IS THE ABILITY TO RULE AND REIGN IN LIFE – the most important thing in life. More important than gold, silver or precious jewels.

The First Key: Praise and Worship.

"And to the angel of the church in Philadelphia write, 'These things says He who is holy, He who is true, "He who has <u>the key of David</u>, He who opens and no one shuts, and shuts and no one opens": "I know your works. See, I have set

before you an open door, and no one can shut it; for you have a little strength, have kept My word, and have not denied My name." (Revelation 3:7-8)

So, what is the key of David? It is praise and worship. David not only wrote most of the Psalms, but when he played the harp, the demonic spirit oppressing Saul would depart. Saul's servants recognised it as a tormenting spirit and asked for a man to play the harp to relieve him. That was David, who was a young, teenage boy at this time.

"Let our master now command your servants, who are before you, to seek out a man who is a skillful player on the harp. And it shall be that he will play it with his hand, when the distressing spirit from God is upon you, and you shall be well." (1Samuel 16:14)

"And so it was, whenever the spirit from God was upon Saul, that David would take a harp and play it with his hand. Then Saul would become refreshed and well, and the distressing spirit would depart from him." (1Samuel 16:23)

Let me explain 'the spirit of God that distressed him'. Here we have King Saul, who had rebelled against God and disobeyed the command of Samuel to wait for him. It resulted in the Spirit of God leaving him (v14), and he had opened himself up to a tormenting spirit. Or God allowed him to be tormented because of his disobedience, which can open the door to the demonic around our lives.

Praise opens the door to peace and victory in your life. Many times, when the Israelites went into battle, the musicians and singers went first, which opened the doorway to victory. We know in Acts 16, that when Paul and Silas were in prison they sang hymns to God. All the prisoners were listening. God sent an earthquake that caused their chains to fall off, the prison doors to open and the jailer to ask how to be saved. Here praise and worship opened the door to salvation for the jailer and his whole household!

> *"But at midnight Paul and Silas were praying and singing hymns to God, and the prisoners were listening to them. Suddenly there was a great earthquake, so that the foundations of the prison were shaken; and immediately all the doors were opened and everyone's chains were loosed." (Acts 16:25-26)*

Secondly, You Need to Know the Key of Authority.

Jesus has all authority in heaven and on earth (Matthew 28:18). All the authority we have comes from Him and His Word and His blood. In Luke 9:1-2, He gave authority and power to the twelve apostles.

> *"Then He called His twelve disciples together and gave them power and authority over all demons, and to cure diseases. He sent them to preach the kingdom of God and to heal the sick."*

Then in Luke 10:1-2 He gave power and authority to the 70 other disciples. He sent them out 'two by two' to the places He was about to go to. In verse 9 He said, *"And heal the sick there and say to them 'the Kingdom of God has come near to you."*

> *"I have given you authority to trample on serpents and scorpions and over all the work of the enemy and nothing shall by any means hurt you."* (verse 19)

This is the promise of God. There is no need to be afraid when confronting demon spirits. Instead, just take authority over them. The Holy Spirit inside you is greater than any demon spirit that might manifest. Every believer needs to know that his/her identity is in Christ (born again Son/Daughter of God) who has the authority of the Father to work IN HIS SON'S NAME.

The Third Key is The Anointing.

Anointing, *mashach* in Hebrew, means to smear, or cover in oil. It relates to a person or object. All of the articles in the temple were anointed along with the Kings, Priests and prophets.

We know from Psalm 23:5, the head was anointed with oil, so their 'cup could overflow. The word 'head' in Hebrew (Rosh) means the leader, the top, the person in authority.

> *"But my horn You have exalted like a wild ox; I have been anointed with fresh oil." (Psalm 92:10)*

The anointing oil was made up of four ingredients that were added to a hin of olive oil (one and a half gallons or five point seven litres). The first ingredient was myrrh, which means **purity,** the second, cinnamon, which represents **obedience** (to obey is better than sacrifice"), the third was calamus (cane), as it required a **purging or cleansing** before it could be used, while the fourth is cassia, which came from the bark of a tree. It speaks of **humility,** as the bark had to be 'stripped away' to be used.

Isaiah 11:1: There are seven Anointings of the Spirit of God. This resembles the Jewish Menorah or candlestick. Jesus represents the middle or main candlestick to which all the others face. As Hebrew is written backwards, we look at them from right to left - wisdom and understanding at the top, then counsel and might, and then knowledge and the fear of the Lord. These are all specific anointings of the Lord Jesus Christ. Jesus means Yeshua or salvation, but Christ means Messiah or the Anointed one.

> *"There shall come forth a Rod from the stem of Jesse, And a Branch shall grow out of his roots. The Spirit of the Lord shall rest upon Him, The Spirit of wisdom and understanding, The Spirit of counsel and might, The Spirit of knowledge and of the fear of the Lord."* (Isaiah 11:1-2)

> *"The Spirit of the Lord GOD is upon Me, Because the LORD has <u>anointed Me</u> To preach good tidings to the poor; He has sent Me to heal the broken hearted, To proclaim liberty to the captives, And the opening of the prison to those who are bound; To proclaim the acceptable year of the LORD* And the day of vengeance of our God." (Isaiah 61:1-2)

It is the anointing that breaks the yokes; because of the anointing oil (Isaiah 10:27). This includes patterns of sin, addictions and demonic torment that can all be broken by the power of the Holy Spirit and the anointing which comes from Him. We have an anointing from the Holy Spirit.

> *"But you have an anointing from the Holy One, and you know all things." (1John 2:20)*
>
> *"But the anointing which you have received from Him abides in you, and you do not need that anyone teach you; but as the same anointing teaches you concerning all things, and Isaiah true, and is not a lie, and just as it has taught you, you will abide in Him."* (1 John 2:27)

The Fourth Key is Prayer with Fasting

Also, you can break yokes by fasting (Isaiah 58:6). This enables people caught in sinful cycles of lust, anger, hatred, jealousy, etcera to be set free, including from all addictions. It enables people who have demonic or tormenting spirits to be set free from all the works of the enemy. Fasting also involves prayer. Without prayer, fasting is only a diet!

> *"Is this not the fast that I have chosen:*
> *To loose the bonds of wickedness,*

To undo the heavy burdens,
To let the oppressed go free,
And that you break every yoke?" (Isaiah 58:6)

If you have yokes of bondage or any addiction, fasting can be a powerful way to help break that cycle. We know that the disciples had authority over the demon spirits (Luke 10:17), but one day a woman brought a boy to them and they could not cast it out. (You can read the story in Matthew 17:14-21; Mark 9:14-29 and Luke 9:37-42). Matthew calls it an epileptic, lunatic spirit, Mark calls it a deaf and dumb spirit and Luke called it an unclean spirit. We know it had been afflicting him from childhood, so it was very well established. Jesus told them they could not cast it out because of <u>their unbelief</u>. Also, He said this kind only goes out **by prayer and fasting!**

> *"So, Jesus said to them, "Because of your unbelief; for assuredly, I say to you, if you have faith as a mustard seed, you will say to this mountain, 'Move from here to there,' and it will move; and nothing will be impossible for you. However, this kind does not go out except* **by prayer and fasting." (Matthew 17:20-21)**

There are many different ways to fast. A Biblical fast usually involves denying the 'flesh' of food, and /or water, or as in the 'Daniel fast', of meat and strong drink. Instead, he ate vegetables and drank water. Daniel chose not to defile himself by eating what was unclean meat.

> *"I ate no pleasant food, no meat or wine came into my mouth, nor did I anoint myself at all, till three whole weeks were fulfilled."* (Daniel 10:3)

We also have the illustration from the book of Esther when she and her maidens fasted for three days before she went to the King (which was not allowed) and said "if I perish, I perish" (Esther 4:16).

Many times, people will fast one meal a day, or only eat once a day. There are no rules or regulations. You do what you feel God wants and also what your body can handle. For those with medical conditions, you should consult your doctor first. Some people will fast sweet things while others fast social media as this is 'pleasurable' to them. The idea is to deny yourself to pray and seek God.

When you decide to fast, **it is important to know why you are fasting and what you are fasting for.** Many people will fast for their family members to come into the Kingdom. Others will fast for specific direction and the call of God on their lives, for a relationship/work problem, for a mission work, or maybe a personal thing like finances or starting a business. Certainly, you should seek God for your marriage partner or if you are planning to move locations. In fact, for any major decision you are facing.

These four things, praise/worship, authority, the anointing and prayer with fasting. These are all keys freely given to us. They are not like 'fruit of the spirit' that you have to grow and develop within your life. Of course, both the keys and the fruit require you to walk in faith, so you can grow into maturity.

Chapter 5
Understanding the Kingdom through Jesus' Parables

Jesus taught <u>Parables of the Kingdom</u>, starting in Matthew 13 with the Parable of the Four Types of Soil. A parable is an earthly story but with a heavenly meaning. We see how the disciples came and asked Him the meaning of each parable. He told them in Matthew 13:11 that ***"It was given to them (the disciples) to know the mysteries of the kingdom of heaven, but to them (the multitude) it was not given."*** He went on to say the reason.

Then Jesus quoted from the book of Isaiah saying, *"they <u>hear</u> but don't understand, <u>See</u>, but don't perceive (discern), for their hearts have grown dull, their ears are hard of hearing, and they have closed their eyes (to truth), lest they see with their eyes and hear with their ears and understand with their hearts and turn (repent) that I should heal them"* (Matthew 13:13-15).

In the Gospel of Mark 4:12 He adds the words, ***"turn and be forgiven."*** Clearly the purpose of teaching in a parable was that they would hear, see (perceive) and understand so transformation could come into their lives. Without understanding, there is no change. It's like speaking to someone in a foreign language. They hear you but have no idea what you are speaking! So how can you reply? How can you put something into action?

Verse 11 of Matthew 13:

> *"It was given to them (the disciples) to know the mysteries of the kingdom of heaven, but to them (the multitude) it was not given."*

It is for YOU TO KNOW and whoever wants more truth!

> *"Ask, and it will be given to you; seek, and you will find; knock, and it will be opened to you. For everyone who asks receives, and he who seeks finds, and to him who knocks it will be opened."* (Matthew 7:7-8)

So, it is for us to seek that we might know the truth, for truly the mysteries of the Kingdom have been given to us.

Section One - The Parables of the Seed and of Harvest

- Parable of the Four Soils (Foundational Parable)
- The Wheat and the Tares
- The Mustard Seed
- The Leaven
- The Treasure Hidden in a Field
- The Pearl of Great Price
- The Dragnet

Firstly, the Foundational Parable: The Four Soils— Matthew 13:1-9; 18-23.

The seed was always **good**, representing **the Word of God**. However, it fell on **four different types of soil**, resulting in **four different outcomes**. It was ONLY the good ground that produced a **harvest** – of thirty, sixty and one hundredfold.

The first soil was **the wayside** (verse 4). It was hard like a track that an animal has passed over many times pressing the soil down. This meant the seed could not penetrate into the soil, but just lay on the top so the birds of the air came and ate it. Jesus explained to them (v19) that this was when they did not understand what they heard and the Devil came and snatched it away. So, there was **no fruit**. It has been said that when you do a work for God, the Enemy will try and snatch the seed. That is because that seed has great ability to multiply.

Secondly, the seed fell into **stony ground** where there was not much earth. So immediately it sprang up, but soon withered in the hot sun as there was no depth of earth (verse 20). Jesus explained this person received the Word with joy, but could not endure for long as he had NO ROOT IN HIMSELF or even any depth of the Word of God. This meant that when difficulties or persecution came, he stumbled because of the word (verse 21-22). You could say he had no inner strength to fight when things got hard. This is like many passive Christians. They allow the Devil access to their lives in many ways and bear **no fruit.**

The third time the seed fell among **thistles,** which grew up and choked the Word (verse 7). The thistles represent the cares of this life and the deceitfulness of riches (chasing after money and possessions), choking the Word and therefore being unfruitful (verse 22). How many times have you been too busy to attend to spiritual matters? I think we can all be guilty of that at times. Just notice when that happens, you are **UNFRUITFUL**.

The fourth soil was the **good soil**. It yielded a crop: thirty, sixty and one hundredfold (v 8). It goes on to say this was the person who hears the Word and understood it. This parable concludes with the words *"He who has ears to hear, let him hear"!* In other words—hear, understand

and act upon. It adds emphasis to the importance of the meaning and listening, understanding and obeying its intent.

This is important to notice here, that only the seed that fell on good soil reproduced. It did not double! Instead, it produced 30, 60 and 100 times! This is a picture of our hearts that can soften, open, and receive the Word of God and understand it.

The book of James goes on to tell us not only must we HEAR and UNDERSTAND, but also ACT upon it. If you don't act upon the Word, there will be <u>no fruit in your life</u>. You will just be like the man who "looks in a mirror and sees what sort of man he is, but does nothing about it."

> *"For if anyone is a hearer of the word and not a doer, he is like a man observing his natural face in a mirror; for he observes himself, goes away, and immediately forgets what kind of man he was. But he who looks into the perfect law of liberty and continues in it, and is not a forgetful hearer but <u>a doer of the work</u>, this one <u>will be blessed</u> in what he does."* (James 1:23-27)

We have already talked about showing our faith by our works. In other words, there should be something that sets us apart from other people. A very good example, if in a disaster like a flood, famine, earthquake etc. If you study history, you will see it was the Christians that came to the rescue and brought aid, workers, funds, whatever was needed. I remember the Guatemalan earthquake in 1976. It was a 7.5 magnitude and brought much damage. I was working in World Vision at the time. Much aid was sent to the country including nurses and doctors. Today, largely as a result, well over 70% of the nation are Christian.

There is a saying: *"When people see your good works, they will glorify God."* Let us strive to glorify God in all that we do.

In Luke 6:42-45 it says, *"a good tree does not bear bad fruit. A tree is known by its fruit. You cannot get figs from thorns or grapes from brambles. A good man brings forth treasure out of his heart and an evil man from evil. Out of the heart the mouth speaks."* In other words, the fruit we produce in our lives, depends on the condition of our heart, whether it is good – positive, or evil – toxic to ourselves and others. What you meditate on will determine what is in your heart.

> *"Finally, brethren, whatever things are true, whatever things are noble, whatever things are just, whatever things are pure, whatever things are lovely, whatever things are of good report, if there is any virtue and if there is anything praiseworthy—meditate on these things."* (Philippians 4:8-9)

The Parable of the Wheat and the Tares
(Matthew 13:24-30; 36-43)

This parable carries on from the Parable of the Four soils.

The Kingdom of heaven is like a field where a man sowed good seed, but while he slept an enemy came and sowed tares (weeds). As the grain sprouted it produced a crop. Both wheat and tares grew so the two could be seen side by side. The servants came and asked if they should pull out the weeds but the master replied, *"no because he would also uproot the good plants."* Instead, he should wait until harvest, then <u>gather the tares first into a bundle to be burnt</u> and put the wheat into the barn.

The disciples came asking for the interpretation of this parable. Jesus replied: The Son of Man (Jesus) sows the good seed (wheat – sons of the Kingdom) into a field (which represents the world), but then the Enemy (the Devil) comes and sows the tares (sons of the wicked one). The harvest is the end of the age and the reapers are angels. The Son of Man will send out His angels to **first** gather out of the Kingdom, <u>all things that offend</u> and belong to the Devil, all those that <u>practise lawlessness</u> and they will be thrown into the fire. There will be wailing and gnashing of teeth. Then the righteous will shine forth as the sun in the Kingdom of their Father.

It's very interesting when you see a picture of wheat, golden and ripe for harvest. It always bends over in the wind—like a picture of submission. However, the tares stand up strong and tall like a rebellious and proud person who will not bend his will. Wheat is brown when it is ripe, but the tares are taller and dark brown or black and easily seen.

It is interesting that the tares and all <u>things that offend</u> are gathered first. Things that offend are works of lusts of the flesh, jealousy, anger, hatred, sexual immorality, unforgiveness, witchcraft, lying, etc. These are 'plants' in our life that are toxic plants that need to be removed. Jesus said *it's not the food you eat that defiles but the unclean things in the heart that come out of the mouth* (Matthew 15:11).

In Hebrews 12:15, it talks about a **root of bitterness** that springs up and defiles you. Clearly, this also needs to be pulled out before the poison spreads.

We see how the parables contain hidden mysteries. **So, what is the hidden mystery of this parable?**

Humility is one of the keys of the Kingdom

> *"The reward for humility and the fear of the Lord is riches, honour and life."* (Proverbs 22:4)

Pursuing Righteousness

We start our prayer, "Our Father, who art in heaven, hallowed (holy, honoured, reverenced) is your name! (Matthew 6:9). So, clearly humility is linked to the fear of the Lord, which is the beginning of wisdom and knowledge. It literally means to have your face down in the dirt, bowing in submission and authority, without personal pride.

Psalm 10:12 says *"Do not forget the humble,"* and v17-18 goes on to say, *"You have heard the desire of the humble; you will prepare their heart; you will cause your ear to hear, to do justice to the fatherless and the oppressed, that the man of the earth may oppress no more."*

God hears the cry of the humble and prepares their heart to do justice in the earth. Jesus taught us not to '*Lord it over others'* and that *'a disciple is not above his teacher or a servant above his master."* Jesus Himself, modelled servant leadership.

In Matthew 18:2-5, Jesus set a child in their midst, telling them that unless they *'became as a little child, they could not enter the Kingdom of heaven. For whoever HUMBLES himself, as a child, is greatest in the Kingdom'*.

We also read in Philippians how Jesus did not exalt Himself. Rather, He humbled Himself, in obedience, even to the point of being crucified, and let God exalt Him in due time.

"Who, being in the form of God, did not consider it robbery to be equal with God, but made Himself of no reputation, taking the form of a bondservant, and coming in the likeness of men. And being found in appearance as a man, He humbled Himself and became obedient to the point of death, even the death of the cross. Therefore, God also has highly exalted Him and given Him the name which is above every name." (Philippians 2:6-9)

You might ask why does God hate pride so much?

Pride, of course, is the opposite of humility. Proverbs 6:16 says there are six things God hates. The first thing is a proud or haughty look. What does this mean? It means you consider yourself superior to someone, so that you look down upon them, even to disdain them or show contempt for them.

We also know, *"God resists the proud, but gives grace to the humble"* (James 4:6; 1 Peter 5:5-6). We have a choice to evoke God's favour or His displeasure.

The reason is that Lucifer, who was God's anointed Cherub in the Garden of Eden, clothed in the beauty of every precious stone, was perfect until iniquity was found in him. Ezekiel 28:17 tells us *"His heart was lifted up (means became proud) because of his beauty"* so he was cast out of heaven. We also see in Isaiah 14:14 where he says *"I will ascend into heaven, I will exalt my throne above the stars of God, I will also sit on the mount of the congregation on the farthest sides of the north; I will ascend above the heights of the clouds; I will be like the MOST HIGH."*

I, I, I. Lucifer, now named Satan, fell from grace and a most prominent place in heaven because of PRIDE. He wanted to exalt himself to be as God (and still does by the way, so be aware of his schemes). Therefore, we must be on guard against pride. The key to dealing with pride, is putting on humility (Colossians 2:12). That is why it is an important character quality of the Kingdom.

This parable is about the End of the Age—that is the Coming of Jesus and the time before His return. Many people, I believe, have wrongly believed in a secret rapture of the body of Christ, where believers are taken first, free from any trouble or persecution or tribulation. However, we can clearly see from this parable the wicked are taken first and thrown into the fire (hell, all the things that produce no fruit) but the righteous remain. I am not saying that God will not protect the body during the Great Tribulation, as I believe He will, but it will be like it was in Goshen in the book of Exodus. If they stayed in Goshen, they were protected, but if they went back into Egypt, the plagues would come on them. God made a *'distinction between the Children of God and between the Egyptians'*. I believe it will be similar to that. As long as we follow the leading of the Holy Spirit and what God is saying, I believe there will be a protection for His people. We saw this in the days of Hitler, where some heard the Holy Spirit and departed for America. Others who stayed behind faced the holocaust. Therefore, it is essential to hear and follow the direction of the Holy Spirit.

"A thousand may fall at your side, and ten thousand at your right hand; But it shall not come near you. Only with your eyes shall you look, And see the reward of the wicked." (Psalm 91:7-8)

We know the saints of old were persecuted, suffered stoning, crucified, put into boiling oil, tar and feathered and thrown to the lions. So, like Daniel in the lion's den, some were saved and some suffered for the sake of the Lord (see Hebrews 11:35-40), those of whom 'the world was not worthy.'

There is a special call for some people, as there is a crown for suffering. There is also a baptism of suffering, but not all are called to walk in it. We see in Revelation 3:8-11 the persecuted church of Smyrna, that they would face tribulation ten days, but *"be faithful unto death and I will give you the crown of life."*

Being Unfruitful or Barren

Many people have no fruit in their lives. We know from John 15 that Jesus is the vine and we are the branches and as we abide in HIM we will bear fruit. His life flows through us to bring life to others. **We cannot do anything without Him,** and His life flowing in and through us. This is how we bear fruit (John 15:5-8).

Abide in Me, and I in you. As the branch cannot bear fruit of itself, unless it abides in the vine, neither can you, unless you abide in Me.

> *"I am the vine, you are the branches. He who abides in Me, and I in him, bears much fruit; for without Me you can do nothing. If anyone does not abide in Me, he is cast out as a branch and is withered; and they gather them and throw them into the fire, and they are burned. If you abide in Me, and My words abide in you, you will ask what you desire, and it shall be done for you. By this My Father is glorified, that you bear much fruit; so, you will be My disciples."*

Fruitfulness comes from abiding in the vine.

The branches that have no fruit and are separated are thrown into the fire to be burned. So, make sure you are attached to Christ – in HIM. Christianity is not a religion, but a relationship with the King of kings and Lord of lords. It is an awesome privilege that He would choose us to be His friends, His co-labourers, His disciples.

The five foolish virgins who were not ready for the wedding feast. They were told *"I never knew you"*

(Matthew 25:12). The word *know*, means intimacy. So, clearly knowing Christ is very important.

The Parable of the Mustard Seed (Matthew 13:31)

"Another parable He put forth to them, saying: "The kingdom of heaven is like a mustard seed, which a man took and sowed in his field, which indeed is the least of all the seeds; but when it is grown it is greater than the herbs and becomes a tree, so that the birds of the air come and nest in its branches."

This is a very short parable but shows us the Kingdom, like a mustard seed starts very small, but can enlarge to go into all the world. We know from Matthew 17:20 that the mustard seed is about FAITH.

"So, Jesus said to them, "Because of your unbelief (you could not cast out the demon from the boy); for assuredly, I say to you, if you have <u>faith as a mustard seed</u>, you will say to this mountain, 'Move from here to there,' and it will move; and <u>nothing will be impossible for you</u>."

So, when we put the two Scriptures together, we see that faith has to grow, even big, like a tree where birds can nest. Then with strong faith, nothing will be impossible in the Kingdom of God.

Mark 4:26-29 The seed contains a cycle. First it must die. Then it puts forth the blade. The ear (or head) then the full head of grain appears and we must wait until it ripens. Finally, you can put in the sickle to harvest the grain as it is ripe and ready for harvest.

We are also told the seed has to die to bring forth life.

> *"Most assuredly, I say to you, unless a grain of wheat falls into the ground and dies, it remains alone; but if it dies, it produces much grain."* (John 12:24)

This follows with three very short parables (The Leaven, the Hidden Treasure and the Pearl of Great Price).

Parable of the Leaven (v33)

> *Another parable He spoke to them: "The kingdom of heaven is like leaven, which a woman took and hid in three measures of meal till it was all leavened."*

We know the leaven is put into bread to make it rise. It literally grows, just like the kingdom is meant to spread throughout the world. *"Go into all the world and preach the Gospel to every creature*" (Mark 16:15). That's why Jesus said "Let your Kingdom come" (Matthew 6:10) – let it advance into all the world and expand like the parable of the leaven.

The Parable of the Hidden Treasure (v44)

> *"Again, the kingdom of heaven is like treasure hidden in a field, which a man found and hid; and for joy over it he goes and sells all that he has and buys that field.*

This means <u>the Kingdom of heaven is so valuable</u> that a person would sell everything to obtain it. The Kingdom of Jesus Christ is the hidden treasure we are to search for.

In the middle East, as well as the wild west, they would hide their valuables in the field to protect them from robbers. The field is the world. Jesus bought the field with His blood.

The next parable is very similar.

The Parable of the Pearl of Great Price (v45-46)

"Again, the kingdom of heaven is like a merchant seeking beautiful pearls, who, when he had found one pearl of great price, went and sold all that he had and bought it.

The Kingdom of Heaven is what we all long for—a place of peace, love, joy, righteousness, no pain, suffering, abuse or evil. A Perfect world. That's why in these two parables a man would sell everything to obtain it. The Kingdom of Heaven is <u>"within us"</u>! A pearl is very <u>valuable.</u> It is made through irritation of a grain of sand within the oyster. That irritation causes the beautiful pearl to be formed. So, with us, also, beauty within is caused by trials, difficulties and irritations.

2Corinthians 4:7, *"We have this treasure with us."*

The Parable of the Dragnet (v47-52)

This parable is about the dragnet cast into the sea that gathered all kinds (of fish) and when brought to the shore, the good were put into vessels and the bad were thrown away. The Bible says this refers to the end of the age. Angels will come forth to separate the wicked (people) from the just (people) who will be cast into the lake of fire, where there is weeping and gnashing of teeth.

We know in the Bible, fish refers to <u>believers</u> and the sea refers to the <u>nations</u>. This is a parable that speaks (I believe) of an 'end time harvest' of many—some good, some bad, that will flood into the kingdom. I actually had a vision in a prayer meeting recently. I saw waves of the sea coming in with many faces in the waves. A great harvest of people. Then I saw the Lord sitting on the beach and sorting the fish, the good from the bad. This parable ends with Jesus asking if they have understood.

> *Then He said to them, "Therefore every scribe instructed concerning the kingdom of heaven is like a householder who brings out of his treasure things new and old."* (v52)

This implies there are treasures both new and old. Many Christians hardly ever read the Old Testament but there are many treasures obtained in it that will make the treasures of the New Testament much more real and meaningful. To understand the new, you must understand the old, as that is the foundation the new is built upon.

Section Two – Parables of Prayer/Persistence and Judgement

- The Unjust Judge and the Persistent Woman

- Judgement of the Sheep and Goat Nations
- The Parable of the Rich Man and Lazarus
- The Parable of the Unforgiving Servant

The Parable of the Unjust Judge and the Persistent Widow.

*"Then He spoke a parable to them, that men **always ought to pray and not lose heart,** saying: 'There was in a certain city a judge who did not fear God nor regard man. Now there was a widow in that city; and she came to him, saying, 'Get justice for me from my adversary.' And he would not for a while; but afterward he said within himself, 'Though I do not fear God nor regard man, yet because this widow troubles me I will avenge her (do justice for her), lest by her continual coming she weary me.'"* (Luke 18:1-5)

It starts by saying this parable is that men ought to **pray always and not lose heart.** It speaks of an unrighteous judge who is plagued by a widow asking for justice who is very **persistent**. He will not heed her demands at first, but because she continues to pester him, he gives in, so he is not tired out.

We know every parable has a spiritual meaning and it tells us at the beginning it is about prayer and not giving up. Let's turn to 1Thessalonians 5:16-18.

> *"Rejoice always, **pray without ceasing**, in everything give thanks; for this is the will of God in Christ Jesus for you."*

Here there is a clear pattern—rejoice (Praise and worship)—<u>prayer with thanksgiving.</u> This clearly means praying without giving up. So, this parable is about prayer. Start with rejoicing and giving thanks <u>then make your requests known to God</u>. Don't be anxious about anything, but as you pray, receive God's peace.

> *"Be anxious for nothing, **but in everything by prayer and supplication, with thanksgiving,** let your requests be made known to God; and the peace of God, which surpasses all understanding, will guard your hearts and minds through Christ Jesus."* (Philippians 4:6-7)

There is a link between prayer and giving thanks. Supplication is making prayer for your own needs, which we are told to do. (Intercession is when you pray for someone or something else.) We are told to give thanks to God in **ALL** things.

> *"...giving thanks always for all things to God the Father in the name of our Lord Jesus Christ."* (Ephesians 5:20)

Pursuing Righteousness

In 1Corinthians 9:24-27 it talks about running to receive a prize. Only one runner can win. Those who compete are <u>temperate</u> or <u>self-controlled</u> and <u>disciplined</u>. Self-control is one of the nine fruits of the Spirit (Galatians 5:22). People who are disciplined do not easily give up, but press through the pain and difficulties to win the prize.

We know every athlete training for the Olympics spends hours, days, months in training. They endure pain and setbacks, but don't give up. They press through the difficulties as they have a goal. That goal is a gold medal and to represent their nation before the world.

"Do you not know that those who run in a race all run, but one receives the prize? Run in such a way that you may obtain it. And everyone who competes for the prize is ***temperate (self-controlled)*** *in all things. Now they do it to obtain a perishable crown, but we for an imperishable crown. Therefore, I run thus: not with uncertainty. Thus, I fight: not as one who beats the air. But I* ***discipline*** *my body and bring it into subjection, lest, when I have preached to others, I myself should become disqualified."* (1Corinthians 9:24)

"Therefore we also, since we are surrounded by so great a cloud of witnesses, let us lay aside every weight, and the sin which so easily

*ensnares us, and let us **run with endurance the race that is set before us**, looking unto Jesus, the author and finisher of our faith, who for the joy that was set before Him endured the cross, despising the shame, and has sat down at the right hand of the throne of God."* (Hebrews 12:1-3)

There is a race of faith that we run. It's called the Christian life. We have **to run with endurance (not giving up)**. There is always a contention between the flesh and the spirit. The flesh easily gives up. Therefore, we must be on guard against giving up, or giving in to pain and difficulty. We need to keep our eyes on the goal – our heavenly reward for a race well run and **develop strength to carry on.**

> *"But you**, be strong and do not let your hands be weak (do not give up)**, for your work shall be rewarded!"* (2Chronicles 15:7)

> *"And let us **not grow weary** while doing good, for in due season we shall reap if we **do not lose heart.**"* (Galatians 6:9)

It is so easy to get tired and give up and not be persistent. Here it says don't lose heart. In Greek, that means to unloose, to have your strength go away, to grow weak or to be faint-hearted. We know before Jesus went to the

Cross, He asked his disciples to pray. But they were tired and fell asleep. Jesus said:

> *"Then He came to the disciples and found them sleeping, and said to Peter, "What! Could you not watch with Me one hour?*" (Matthew 26:40)

In the book of Deuteronomy 20:6-9, those whoever were fearful or faint-hearted for the battle were told to return home lest he make his brothers also faint-hearted (afraid or dismayed).

The Apostle Paul talks of weakness too, but in a different way. He says **'when we are weak, then we are strong'** because we are relying upon God and not ourselves. He says God's grace is sufficient or enough to help us through the difficult times.

> *"And He said to me, "My grace is sufficient for you, for My strength is made perfect in weakness." Therefore, most gladly I will rather boast in my infirmities, that the power of Christ may rest upon me. Therefore, I take pleasure in infirmities, in reproaches, in needs, in persecutions, in distresses, for Christ's sake.* ***For when I am weak, then I am strong."*** (2Corinthians 12:9-10)

So, in times of sickness, when people have spoken badly about you, when you have a need or are persecuted or in distress, that's the time to draw on God's strength to get you through.

Joshua was told a number of times to be **strong and courageous** (**not faint-hearted or discouraged**). Discouraged means your courage has gone (Joshua 1:6,7,9). Fear will take our courage and our strength. Also, to be dismayed means to feel concern or distress.

> *"**Fear not**, for I am with you; **Be not dismayed**, for I am your God. I will **strengthen** you, Yes, I will **help** you, I will uphold you with My righteous right hand." (Isaiah 41:10)*

It continues in Joel 3:9-10 saying for the mighty men to wake up and prepare for war. They are to strengthen themselves to face the battle and not be faint-hearted.

> *"Proclaim this among the nations: "Prepare for war! **Wake up the mighty men**, **Let**, all the men of war draw near, Let them come up. Beat your plowshares into swords And your pruning hooks into spears; Let the weak say, '**I am strong.**'"*

Do you notice the word 'let'? It is a command to act. Another thought similar to **persisting is overcoming.** It means to **be victorious** through every difficulty, battle, trial and not give up but fulfil God's plan and purpose. We know Jesus overcame the world (John16:33). Also we are more than conquerors in Christ Jesus (Romans 8:37). We see this word used a lot in the letters of the Apostle John to the seven churches in Revelation two and three.

Revelation 2:7 (Church of Ephesus, the loveless church) *"**To him who overcomes** I will give to eat from the tree of life, which is in the midst of the Paradise of God."*

Revelation 2:11 (Church of Smyrna, the Persecuted church) *"**He who overcomes** shall not be hurt by the second death."*

Revelation 2:17 (Church of Pergamos, the Comprising Church) "**He who overcomes** *I will give some of the hidden manna to eat and on the stone a new name written which no one knows, except him who receives it."*

Revelation 2:25-26 (Church of Thyatira – the Corrupt church) *"But, **hold fast** what you have till I come. And **he who overcomes**, and keeps My works until the end, to him I will give power over the nations."*

Revelation 3:5 (Church of Sardis, the Dead Church) *"He who **overcomes** shall be clothed in white garments, and I will not blot out his name from the Book of Life; but I will confess his name before My Father and before His angels."*

Revelation 3:10-12 (Church of Philadelphia, The Faithful Church) "*He who overcomes, I will make him a pillar in the temple of My God, and he shall go out no more. I will write on him the name of My God and the name of the city of My God, the New Jerusalem, which comes down out of heaven from My God. And I will write on him My new name.*"

Revelation 3:21 (Laodicea, the Lukewarm Church) "*To him who **overcomes** I will grant to sit with Me on My throne, as I also overcame and sat down with My Father on His throne.*"

Every time there is the statement: "*To him who **overcomes**,*" there is a specific promise given. We are told to hold fast, (don't give up) and overcome (remain victorious) until the end, or even unto death.

Finishing well is very important. So many give up along the way. Sometimes men's hearts fail (faint) for fear. Jesus taught in Luke 21:26-28 to "*Look up, because your redemption draws nigh.*" Jesus is returning to end injustice.

In the book of Genesis, Chapter 18, we find a very interesting story that perfectly illustrates persistence. In verse 17, we see God saying, "*will He hide from Abraham what He is doing*"? This is because the outcry of sin and evil had reached God over Sodom and Gomorrah. When God says He is going to destroy these cities, Abraham intercedes. He asks of God, *"Will you destroy the righteous with the wicked? What if there are fifty righteous people?*

So, the LORD said, "If I find in Sodom fifty righteous within the city, then I will spare all the place for their sakes" (v26).

Abraham continues to ask God for forty-five (v28), then forty (v29), then thirty (v30), then twenty (v31). Each time God said He would **not destroy it** for that number of righteous people. Abraham did not give up but asked God one last time. He persevered in his intercession, just like the widow woman **persisted with** the unrighteous judge.

"Then he said, 'Let not the Lord be angry, and I will speak but once more: Suppose ten should be found there?" And He said, "I will not destroy it for the sake of ten.'" (v32)

Let us return to the end of the Parable in Luke 18:6-8:

"Then the Lord said, "Hear what the unjust judge said. And shall God not avenge His own elect who cry out day and night to Him, though He bears long with them? I tell you that He will avenge them speedily. Nevertheless, when the Son

of Man comes, will He really find faith on the earth?"

There is a Day of Judgment coming, so we need to be ready and found with faith, expectant. We know that Cain killed his brother Abel (who was the first prophet in the Bible), and his blood cried out to God from the ground (Genesis 4:10; Matthew 23:35). In Hebrews 12:24 it tells us that "Jesus' blood speaks louder than Abel's. In Revelation 6:10-11 it says:

*"And they cried with a loud voice, saying, "How long, O Lord, holy and true, until **You judge and avenge our blood** on those who dwell on the earth?" Then a white robe was given to each of them; and it was said to them that they should <u>rest a little while longer</u>, until both the number of their fellow servants and their brethren, who would be killed as they were, was <u>completed.</u>*

God is the righteous judge of all the earth. His throne is built upon righteousness and justice (Psalm 89:14). Jesus said 'His judgment was just' (John 5:30 and Psalm 96:13), that He is coming to judge the earth.

Parable of the Sheep and Goat Nations

"When the Son of Man comes in His glory, and all the holy angels with Him, then He will sit on the throne of His glory. All the nations will be gathered before Him, and He will separate them one from another, as a shepherd divides his sheep from the goats. And He will set the sheep on His right hand, but the goats on the left. Then the King will say to those on His right hand, 'Come, you blessed of My Father, inherit the kingdom prepared for you from the foundation of the world: for I was hungry and you gave Me food; I was thirsty and you gave Me drink; I was a stranger and you took Me in; I was naked and you clothed Me; I was sick and you visited Me; I was in prison and you came to Me.' (Matthew 25:31-36)

It says when the 'Son of Man comes in His glory with the holy angels' (at the Second Coming) He will sit on the throne of His glory. All the nations will be gathered before Him and He will separate them one from another. He will judge the earth. He will separate the good **nations** from the bad. (It will also be for individuals. Remember the Parable of the Dragnet?) The good nations are called the sheep nations and are put on the right— these will enter into an inheritance of eternal life, while the goat nations/people are put on the left and they will be sent to hell/eternal punishment.

> *"Then the King will say to those on His right hand, 'Come, you blessed of My Father, **inherit the kingdom prepared for you from the foundation of the world:** for I was hungry and you gave Me food; I was thirsty and you gave Me drink; I was a stranger and you took Me in; I was naked and you clothed Me; I was sick and you visited Me; I was in prison and you came to Me.'*
>
> *"Then the righteous will answer Him, saying, 'Lord, when did we see You hungry and feed You, or thirsty and give You drink? When did we see You a stranger and take You in, or naked and clothe You? Or when did we see You sick, or in prison, and come to You?' And the King will answer and say to them, 'Assuredly, I say to you**, inasmuch as you did it to one of the least of these My brethren, you did it to Me.'*** (Matthew 25:34-40)

Here we see that there is an inheritance for those who reach out to the hungry, thirsty, strangers and the naked. This is for individuals but also refers to the nations as there are sheep and goat nations. Even if we just helped one person, it is as if we did it to the Lord Himself.

Pursuing Righteousness

"Then He will also say to those on the left hand, 'Depart from Me, you cursed, into the everlasting fire prepared for the devil and his angels: for I was hungry and you gave Me no food; I was thirsty and you gave Me no drink; I was a stranger and you did not take Me in, naked and you did not clothe Me, sick and in prison and you did not visit Me.'

"Then they also will answer Him, saying, 'Lord, when did we see You hungry or thirsty or a stranger or naked or sick or in prison, and did not minister to You?' Then He will answer them, saying, 'Assuredly, I say to you, inasmuch as you did not do it to one of the least of these, you did not do it to Me.' **And these will go away into everlasting punishment, but the righteous into eternal life."**

Here we have a judgment of individuals and nations, based on whether they fed the hungry, gave water to the thirsty, clothed the naked and reached out to strangers (foreigners). Right throughout the Old Testament we see the children of Israel were instructed to look after the poor, widows, orphans and strangers. They were not to harvest the edges of the grain fields, but leave them for the poor and foreigners living among you (Leviticus 23:22). In Deuteronomy 24:19 it specifically says,

"When you reap your harvest in your field, and forget a sheaf in the field, you shall not go back to get it; it shall be for the stranger, the fatherless, and the widow, **that the LORD your God may bless you in all the work of your hands."**

Why is in on the heart of God to look after the poor, widow, orphans and strangers in the land?

1. There is a blessing for those who help the widows, orphans and strangers in the land—that God may bless you in all the work of your hands! (Deuteronomy 24:19)

In Exodus 22:22, they were told not to mistreat widows or orphans or that curse would come back on them. In fact, they were commanded to set aside a tithe of food for widows, orphans and strangers within their gates, that they might come and eat and be satisfied (Deuteronomy 14:29). Today this is like helping solo Mums and blended families.

2. God instituted this so the poor would be looked after, but also so **they would remember that once they were slaves in Egypt,** the poorest of the poor, and God redeemed them from there (Deuteronomy 24:18). God commanded them to do it. It was not an optional extra if they felt like it!

*"But you shall remember that you were a slave in Egypt, and the L*ORD *your God redeemed you from there; therefore, I <u>command</u> you to do this thing."*

3. There is a coming judgement (both of reward for good deeds and punishment for evil deeds).

"*But we know that the judgment of God is according to truth against those who practice such things (Romans 2:2). But in accordance with your hardness and your impenitent heart you are treasuring up for yourself wrath in the day of wrath and revelation of the righteous judgment of God, who <u>"will render to each one according to his deeds"</u>: eternal life to those who by patient continuance in doing good seek for glory, honour, and immortality;(v5-7)…but glory, honour, and peace to everyone who works what is good, to the Jew first and also to the Greek (v10).*

… but to those who are self-seeking and do not obey the truth, but obey unrighteousness— indignation and wrath, tribulation and anguish, on every soul of man who does evil, of the Jew first and also of the Greek (v9-10).

*… in the day (of judgement) when **God will judge***

the secrets of men *by Jesus Christ, according to my gospel.*

In the book of Malachi (the last book of the Old Testament), it warns of coming judgment against sorcerers, adulterers, liars and those who exploit workers, taking advantage of widows and orphans and not showing kindness to the homeless.

> *"And I will come near you for judgment; I will be a swift witness Against sorcerers, against adulterers, against perjurers, <u>Against those who exploit wage earners and widows and orphans, And against those who turn away an alien (foreigner)</u>."*

Because they do not fear Me," *says the* LORD *of hosts"* (Malachi 3:5).

4. Christian Lifestyle

Similarly in the New Testament, we see in Acts 6, they had a feeding programme for the widows. Looking after the poor was something that was part of Christian life. In Galatians 2, we read how Paul went to Jerusalem to discuss with the Apostles His call and ministry to the Gentiles. They gave him the right hand of fellowship (approval of his ministry) but commanded:

"They desired only that we should remember the poor, the very thing which I also was eager to do." (Galatians 2:10)

Then also he said for us to look after the poor, especially believers, <u>and do good works</u>. We know from the book of James, chapter 2, that we show our faith by our good works.

"Therefore, as we have opportunity, let us do good to all, especially to those who are of the household of faith." (Galatians 6:10)

The Rich Man and Lazarus (Luke 16:19 –31)

"There was a certain rich man who was clothed in purple and fine linen and fared sumptuously every day. But there was a certain beggar named Lazarus, full of sores, who was laid at his gate, desiring to be fed with the crumbs which fell from the rich man's table. Moreover, the dogs came and licked his sores. So it was that the beggar died, and was carried by the angels to Abraham's bosom. The rich man also died and was buried. And being in torments in Hades, he lifted up his eyes and saw Abraham afar off, and Lazarus in his bosom.

"Then he cried and said, 'Father Abraham, have mercy on me, and send Lazarus that he may dip the tip of his finger in water and cool my tongue; for I am tormented in this flame.' But Abraham said, 'Son, remember that in your lifetime you received your good things, and likewise Lazarus evil things; but <u>now he is comforted and you are tormented</u>. And besides all this, between us and you there is a <u>great gulf fixed</u>, so that those who want to pass from here to you cannot, nor can those from there pass to us.

"Then he said, 'I beg you therefore, father, that you would send him to my father's house, for I have five brothers, that he may testify to them, lest they also come to this place of torment.' Abraham said to him, 'They have Moses and the prophets; let them hear them.' And he said, 'No, father Abraham; but if one goes to them from the dead, they will repent.' But he said to him, 'If they do not hear Moses and the prophets, neither will they be persuaded though one rise from the dead.'"

Here we see a rich man, who had no regard (mercy) for a man begging at his gate. While he lived on earth, he had everything in the way of worldly goods but spared nothing for the poor man covered in sores who was hungry, wanting even to have some of his crumbs to eat.

However, the poor man had no worldly goods at all. When he died, he went to Abraham's bosom (a picture of heaven) where he was comforted. The rich man went to Hades (hell), where he was in torments (plural). He was able to see Abraham being comforted but not cross over the gulf between them. The Lord refused to send anyone to warn his family, saying they had Moses and the prophets. Jesus said *'if they would not listen to them, neither would they listen, even if someone was raised from the dead'.*

So once again we see there is a judgment based on how we live this life on earth, especially according to how we treat other people.

The Parable of the Unforgiving Servant (Matthew 18:21-35)

This parable begins with a question from Peter asking *'how many times he should forgive his brother?'* Up to seven times? Jesus replied by saying "*seventy times seven.*" In other words, many times!

> *"Therefore, the kingdom of heaven is like a certain king who wanted to settle accounts with his servants. And when he had begun to settle accounts, one was brought to him who owed him ten thousand talents. But as he was not able to pay, his master commanded that he be sold, with*

> *his wife and children and all that he had, and that payment be made. The servant therefore fell down before him, saying, 'Master, have patience with me, and I will pay you all.' Then the master of that servant was moved with compassion, released him, and forgave him the debt."* (Matthew 18:23-27)

Ten thousand talents was a very huge amount. It would have taken his whole life and more to pay it. (One talent was twenty years labour, and he owed ten thousand or about 2 million in today's currency.) So, he was forgiven **this impossible amount.**

> *"But that servant went out and found one of his fellow servants who owed him a hundred denarii; and he laid hands on him and took him by the throat, saying, 'Pay me what you owe!' So, his fellow servant fell down at his feet and begged him, saying, 'Have patience with me, and I will pay you all.' And he would not, but went and threw him into prison till he should pay the debt. So, when his fellow servants saw what had been done, they were very grieved, and came and told their master all that had been done."* (v28-31)

In contrast, the amount this man owed was very small, only about four months wages, but he showed no mercy to his servant.

"Then his master, after he had called him, said to him, 'You wicked servant! I forgave you all that debt because you begged me. Should you not also have had compassion on your fellow servant, just as I had pity on you?' And his master was angry, and delivered him to the torturers until he should pay all that was due to him." (v 32-34)

"So, My heavenly Father also will do to you if each of you, from his heart, does not forgive his brother his trespasses." (v35)

So, forgiveness must be <u>from our heart</u>, and maybe up to 70 times 7 times. This means continually, or as many times as it takes. If we think about our sins being forgiven by God, who sent His beloved son to pay <u>with every last drop of His blood</u> for us (an immeasurable amount, impossible to pay back) and then think about us <u>forgiving our brother</u> – how much more we need to forgive! Their sin can seem so great to us, but in God's eyes, he sees the price He paid for you! I encourage you all to test your hearts to see if you need to forgive someone.

*"Forgive us our sins, as we forgive those who sin against us." (*Matthew 6:12; Luke 11:14)

In the Hebrew language it says, *"In the same way we forgive others, let our sins also be forgiven."* I like this!

It means we forgive first then we are forgiven. Jesus went on to say:

"If we forgive others our sins will also be forgiven. But if we do not forgive others, neither will our sins be forgiven" (Matthew 6:14-15).

These are sobering words and bring out the importance of forgiveness. In 2Corinthians 2:10-11 the Apostle Paul taught that when we forgive others, **it is for our own sake**. "What! You mean if I forgive it helps me? How is this possible?" In verse 11 we see that our unforgiveness gives a foothold or advantage to the Enemy. Let me explain.

If I have unforgiveness and hatred and bitterness in my life, for example, towards my Mother-in-law, that will be like a rope or chain around both of us. IF I DO NOT CHOOSE TO FORGIVE, we will stay chained together for one day, one week, one year, ten years, twenty years, or until the day I die. However, the day I forgive, that chain is broken. She goes free and so do I. Hallelujah.

Let me add that forgiving does not mean I agree with the sin. It just means I release the person to God and will not take revenge. In the Old Testament, if a man took someone's wife, that husband would come after him to kill him. And if you took my donkey, I would take yours. The cycle of a revenge mentality is what fuels anger and generational unforgiveness. You see this in some gangs and indigenous cultures. So, forgiveness is leaving the revenge to God.

There will be a day of judgement for every rape, sexual abuse, murder, cheating, false witness, martyrdom, and every wrong thing done to you. It is not for us to take revenge. Vengeance belongs to God only (Romans 12:13). In Africa, many people had not forgiven for maybe as long as twenty years! It came with a change of mind (heart). Or when they specifically said 'I have decided to forgive." One man said: *"I have made up my mind. I will forgive today"* (after 20 years)!

Section Three – Parables of the Wedding Feasts

- The Great Supper
- The Wedding Banquet
- The Five Wise and Five Foolish Virgins

Parable of the Great Supper Jesus taught in Luke 14:16-24

"Then He said to him, "A certain man gave a great supper and invited many, and sent his servant at supper time to say to those who were invited, 'Come, for all things are now ready.' But they all with one accord began to make excuses. The first said to him, 'I have bought a piece of ground, and I must go and see it. I ask you to

have me excused.' And another said, 'I have bought five yoke of oxen, and I am going to test them. I ask you to have me excused.' Still another said, 'I have married a wife, and therefore I cannot come.' (v16-20)

"*So that servant came and reported these things to his master. Then the master of the house, being angry, said to his servant, 'Go out quickly into the streets and lanes of the city, and bring in here the poor and the maimed and the lame and the blind.' And the servant said, 'Master, it is done as you commanded, and still there is room.' Then the master said to the servant, 'Go out into the highways and hedges, and compel them to come in, **that my house may be filled.** For I say to you that none of those men who were invited shall taste my supper.'"* (v17-24)

A <u>certain man</u> gave a feast and invited many to come, When the servant said all was ready, they gave excuses— I have bought a piece of ground and I must go see it. Another said he had bought five yoke of oxen and had to go test them. Still another said he had married a wife so could not come. So, the master was angry and commanded the servant to go out to the streets and lanes of the city and bring in the poor, crippled, lame, blind. When he said there was <u>still room</u>, he was commanded to go to the highways and hedges and command them to come in so his house could **be full**.

He also said that none of those invited would be able to taste of his supper. (They were not counted worthy, so there was a consequence for making excuses and not making it their priority to go.)

What does this parable mean? It means God wants all to come into the Kingdom. Everyone is welcome. Give and you will be blessed because they cannot repay you**.** But you will be repaid at the resurrection of the just (sheep on the right).

The Parable of the Great Wedding Banquet

There is another parable that is very similar, found in the book of Matthew 22:1-14. In this case **the King** is holding a wedding feast for **His Son** (A picture of the Wedding Supper of the Lamb—Jesus, who is our bridegroom).

Here we see they also made excuses. When the people were invited, they would not come; he was angry and burned their cities. Then he compelled the people in the highways to come instead- the good and the bad, until the wedding hall was full. The King wanted as many to come as possible.

There was one man who came **without a wedding garment** and the King was amazed and said: *"How did you get in here without a wedding garment?"* Either the man was naked (covered with shame) or he didn't have the right wedding clothes (garments of salvation, Isaiah 61:10). He was cast into outer darkness where there is weeping and gnashing of teeth.

In Luke 12:35 it says *"Be dressed for service and keep your lamps burning."* It is important to be clothed in righteousness, be ready (alert, watching and praying) and having lamps burning (The oil of anointing of the Holy Spirit in our lives).

To enter the Kingdom of heaven we know we must be born again. When Nicodemus, a Jewish Pharisee and leader came to Jesus, that is what He told him (John 3:3, "You must be born again'). Jesus said you have to be born of water (natural birth) and born of the Spirit (spiritual birth) to enter the Kingdom of heaven (v5-6). V15 The Son of Man must be lifted up, (crucified), that whoever believes in Him will not perish, but have everlasting life.

Matthew 25 Parable of the 10 Virgins – Five Wise and Five Foolish

These virgins were also waiting for the Bridegroom to come (a picture of Jesus' return). They slept while they were waiting. When the sound was heard at midnight, that He is coming, they rose and trimmed their lamps. The wise had taken extra oil but the foolish were **unprepared**, so their lamps went out. They had to go into town to buy oil, and while they were going the bridegroom came. Those that were **ready** went into the wedding feast and **the door was shut**. (Remember Noah's ark? God shut the door and judgment began.)

Later, the others came begging to be allowed in also. But He answered *"Surely, I do not know you"* (not in relationship with you, no oil = no anointing which we get from the presence of God).

Again, in Matthew 7:21-23 there is a very sobering passage about knowing Him:

> *"Not everyone who says to Me, 'Lord, Lord,' shall enter the kingdom of heaven, **<u>but he who does the will of My Father in heaven</u>**. Many will say to Me in that day, 'Lord, Lord, have we not prophesied in Your name, cast out demons in Your name, and done many wonders in Your name?'*
> *And then I will declare to them, **<u>'I never knew you;</u>** depart from Me, **you who practice lawlessness!'***

Clearly, there is an importance on Knowing Christ and doing His will. Remember Matthew 6:10 *"Let your kingdom come, let your will be done, on earth as it is in heaven."*

You could link this to not looking after the poor, the widows and the orphans as He has commanded. Remember the sheep enter into the Kingdom of God, but the goats do not!

Section Four - Parables on Faithfulness and Stewardship

- **Parable of the Faithful Servant and Evil Servant**
- **Parable of the Unjust Servant (Shrewd Servant)**
- **Parable of the Two Sons – Obedient and Disobedient**
- **Parable of the Minas**
- **Parable of the Talents**

The Parable of the Faithful Servant and the Evil Servant (Luke 12)

This parable begins with the Lord saying *'to be dressed* (your waist girded), *ready with your lamps burning and be like men waiting for the Master to return from the wedding, that when he knocks, you can immediately open'*. It carries on **"Blessed are those servants whom the Master, when he comes, will find watching.** *And you* *yourselves be like men who wait for their master, when he will return from the wedding, that when he comes and knocks, they may open to him **immediately**.* <u>*Blessed are those servants whom the master, when he comes, will find watching.*</u> *Assuredly, I say to you that he will **gird** himself and have them sit down to eat, and will come and serve them." (*Luke 12:35-37)

> *"And if he should come in the second watch, or come in the third watch, and find them so, blessed are those servants. But know this, that if the master of the house had known what hour the thief would come, he would have watched and not allowed his house to be broken into. Therefore, **you also be ready**, for the Son of Man is coming at an hour you do not expect.*" (v 38-40)

The Lord is returning one day soon. The Bible says *"No man knows the day or the hour, not even the angels in heaven, or the Son, but only the Father"* (Matthew 24:36). Therefore, it is imperative that we are clothed (with garments of salvation – girded with truth), ready, (watching and praying) with our lamps burning—not like the five foolish virgins that had no oil.

In verse 41, Peter asked if this parable was just for them (the disciples) or for everyone. Jesus replied:

*"**Who then is that faithful and wise steward**, whom his master will make <u>ruler over his household</u>, to give them their portion of food in due season? Blessed is that servant whom his master will find so doing when he comes. Truly, I say to you that he will make him ruler over all that he has. But if that servant says in his heart, 'My master is delaying his coming,' and begins to beat the male and female servants, and to eat and drink and be drunk, the master of that servant <u>will come on a day when he is not looking for him</u>, and at an hour when he is not aware, and will cut him in two and appoint him his portion with the unbelievers. And that servant who knew his master's will, and did not prepare himself or do according to his will, shall be beaten with many stripes. But he who did not know, yet committed things deserving of stripes, shall be beaten with few. For everyone to whom much is given, from him much will be required; and to whom much has been committed, of him they will ask the more."* (v42-48)

The point of this parable is to be ready and doing the will of the Father when He comes. Remember Matthew 7:21-23, *"not everyone who calls Him Lord will enter the Kingdom, but <u>he who does the will of the Father in Heaven.</u>"* The one who is doing His will, will be made ruler over all He has, because he has been found faithful. He is, in turn, called the faithful and wise steward.

Parable of the Two Sons (Matthew 21:28-31)

"But what do you think? A man had two sons, and he came to the first and said, 'Son, go, work today in my vineyard.' He answered and said, 'I will not,' but afterward he regretted it and went. Then he came to the second and said likewise. And he answered and said, 'I go, sir,' but he did not go. <u>Which of the two did the will of his father?</u>*" They said to Him, "The first." Jesus said to them, "Assuredly, I say to you that tax collectors and harlots enter the kingdom of God before you.*

This is a short parable where one son is obedient to do what the Father (God) wanted, even though he said he wouldn't, he repented and went and did it. The other brother promised to do it but didn't follow through. One was obedient and <u>did the Father's will</u> and one was disobedient. He related this to sinners entering the Kingdom of God more easily, they can more readily know they need God.

The Parable of the Unjust Servant – Parable on Shrewdness (Luke 16:1-13)

This can be a confusing parable if we do not understand the biblical meaning of the word *'shrewd'*. It has both a negative and positive meaning. It basically means **cunning**, as the snake was in the garden, but it also means shrewd in that **you can understand the intentions of evil people and use that to your advantage**. This is what this parable means. The man was about to lose his job people he had not been faithful with his master's money.

> *'He also said to His disciples: "There was a certain rich man who had a steward, and an accusation was brought to him that this man was wasting his goods. So, he called him and said to him, 'What is this I hear about you? <u>Give an account of your stewardship,</u> for you can no longer be steward.'*
>
> *"Then the steward said within himself, 'What shall I do? For my master is taking the stewardship away from me. I cannot dig; I am ashamed to beg. I have resolved what to do, that when I am put out of the stewardship, they may receive me into their houses.'*
>
> *"So, he called every one of his master's debtors to him, and said to the first, 'How much do you owe*

*my master?' And he said, 'A hundred measures of oil.' So, he said to him, 'Take your bill, and sit down quickly and write fifty.' Then he said to another, 'And how much do you owe?' So, he said, 'A hundred measures of wheat.' And he said to him, 'Take your bill, and write eighty.' So, the master commended the unjust steward <u>**because he had dealt shrewdly**</u>. For the sons of this world are more shrewd (discerning of evil) in their generation than the sons of light."*

"And I say to you, make friends for yourselves by unrighteous mammon, that when you fail, they may receive you into an everlasting home." (Luke 16:9)

***"He who is faithful in what is least is faithful also in much**; and he who is unjust in what is least is unjust also in much. Therefore, if you have not been faithful in the unrighteous mammon, who will commit to your trust the true riches?"* (v10-11)

In other words, if you cheat at work, or steal ,God knows. It might be something very small, but will gradually become much larger. Also, if you are faithful with the little things, you can be trusted with much.

> *"And if you have not been faithful in what is another man's, who will give you what is your own?"* (v12)

You need to learn to be faithful looking after someone else's property. That means returning it in a good state, as least as good as what it was when you took it. My pastor used to say he loaned his garden tools to someone, but when they brought them back, they were rusty and not well cared for. Or if someone borrowed his car, it came back dirty, and without petrol. (That's not a good witness.)

> *"No servant can serve two masters; for either he will hate the one and love the other, or else he will be loyal to the one and despise the other. You cannot serve God and mammon."*

God expects us to be faithful and we will be called to give an account. We need to learn to steward God's money well. All we have belongs to Him anyway. There are rewards for those who steward well and punishment for those who don't.

Many Christians consider wealth ungodly, but it is not money, but the *'love of money that is the root of all evil'* (1 Timothy 6:10). It's not about you having money, but does money have you? You cannot love the world and God. Many Christians have one foot in the world and one foot in the church. You cannot walk like that or you will be constantly pulled from one thing to the next and have no stability. This parable is about serving God and not the world as we cannot serve two masters. This parable also teaches us to work hard and use money in such a way that it will give us eternal friends. God expects us to be faithful **as He is faithful.**

> *"For I proclaim the name of the LORD: Ascribe greatness to our God. He is the Rock, His work is perfect; For all His ways are justice, A God of truth and without injustice; Righteous and upright is He." (*Deuteronomy 32:3-4)

In Psalm 92:15 it tells us there **is *no unrighteousness in Him***, and in Psalm 119:89-90 we learn *'His faithfulness lasts for all generations'*.

> *"Forever, O LORD, Your word is settled in heaven. Your faithfulness endures to all generations; You established the earth, and it abides."* (Psalm 119:89-90)
>
> ***"Faithful*** is ***He*** who calls you, and ***He*** also will ***bring it*** to ***pass."*** (1Thessalonians 5:24)

In 1John 1:9 We learn, *'that if we confess our sins, He is faithful and just to forgive us and to cleanse us from all unrighteousness'*.

Then in 2Thessalonians 3:3 *we see, "God is faithful and will establish us and guard us from the Evil One!"*

1Corinthians 4:2 *"It is required that those who have been given a trust must prove faithful."*

In Hebrews 3:2 we read *"Jesus is our High Priest who was faithful to Him who appointed Him, as Moses also was faithful in all his house."* He is our example.

Hebrews 10:23, *"hold fast our confession of faith without wavering, for He who promises is faithful."*

Faithfulness is part of the character of God, so it also needs to be part of our character! It's one of the fruits of the spirit in Galatians 5:22.

This means in our marriages— men not looking at other women and wives respecting their husbands and both keeping their marriage vows (2 Timothy 2:2 – 'flee youthful lusts"). It means being honest in your work— not stealing and working hard—being diligent with the work of our hands (2 Timothy 1:6-7). It also means in ministry, doing what we are called to do—using the gifts that we are given (1Timothy 2:2).

"Commit these to faithful men who are able to teach others." See also the parable of the talents, how we have to use/develop and grow our abilities for the Master's use.

Matthew 20:16 says, *"Many are called, but few are chosen."* Being faithful is a prerequisite for being chosen. That also means faithful with finances.

The Parable of the Minas (Luke 19:11-27)

The principle of stewarding money is further brought out in this parable. A certain nobleman gave one mina to each of ten of his servants and told them to do business until he came. (A mina in today's currency is $10,000 USD). Most people would be expected to make a good return on this amount. However, the truth is, that some people do not know how to invest money. Also, there are many scammers out there who would LOVE to lie and cheat and take your money! Believe me, I know!

> The first man came and said, *'Master, your mina has earned ten minas.'* And he said to him, *'Well done, good servant;* ***because you were faithful in a very little, have authority over ten cities.'*** *And the second came, saying, 'Master, your mina has earned five minas.' Likewise he said to him, '****You also be over five cities*** *'*(v17-19).

Here we have a very interesting thing, The man who gained 10 minas from one mina (increase to $100,000) was given **authority over ten cities**. Likewise, the one who gained five minas ($50,000) was given **authority**

over five cities. This implies that to the degree that you are faithful, is <u>the measure of authority that you are given</u>!

*"Then another came, saying, 'Master, here is your mina, which I have kept put away in a handkerchief. For I feared you, because you are an austere man. You collect what you did not deposit, and reap what you did not sow.' And he said to him, 'Out of your own mouth I will judge you, you <u>wicked servant</u>. You knew that I was an austere man, collecting what I did not deposit and reaping what I did not sow. **Why then did you not put my money in the bank, that at my coming I might have collected it with interest?**'* (It would have been at least $500). So, we know this parable is about stewarding money.

*"And he said to those who stood by, 'Take the mina from him, and give it to him who has ten minas.' (But they said to him, 'Master, he has ten minas.') 'For I say to you, that **to everyone who has will be given**; and from him who does not have, even what he has will be taken away from him. But bring here those enemies of mine, who did not want me to reign over them, and slay them before me.'"*

The one who did not steward the money at all, had it taken off him. Notice it was given to the one who gained ten (stewarded very well). Furthermore, that wicked servant was killed. Let us all learn to be faithful with finances, and may God forgive us when we haven't.

The Parable of the Talents (Gold Coins) (Matthew 25:14-30)

*"For the kingdom of heaven is like a man traveling to a far country, who called his own servants and delivered his goods to them. And to one he gave five talents, to another two, and to another one, to each according to his own ability; and immediately he went on a journey. Then he who had received the five talents went **and traded** with them, and made another five talents. And likewise, he who had received two gained two more also. But he who had received one went and dug in the ground, and hid his lord's money. After a long time, the lord of those servants came and <u>settled accounts</u> with them."* (v14-19)

"So, he who had received five talents came and brought five other talents, saying, 'Lord, you delivered to me five talents; look, I have <u>gained five more</u> talents besides them.' His lord said to him, 'Well done, good and faithful servant; you were <u>faithful over a few things, I will make you ruler over many things. Enter into the joy of your lord.</u>' He also who had received two talents came and said, 'Lord, you delivered to me two talents; look, I have <u>gained two</u> <u>more</u> talents besides them.' His lord said to him, 'Well done, good and faithful servant; you have been faithful over a few things,

I will make you ruler over many things. Enter into the joy of your lord.' (v20-23)

"Then he who had received the one talent came and said, 'Lord, I knew you to be a hard man, reaping where you have not sown, and gathering where you have not scattered seed. And I was afraid, and went and hid your talent in the ground. Look, there you have what is yours.' (v24-25)

"But his lord answered and said to him, 'You <u>wicked and lazy servant</u>, you knew that I reap where I have not sown, and gather where I have not scattered seed. So, you ought to <u>have deposited my money with the bankers</u>, and at my coming I would have received back my own <u>with interest</u>. So take the talent from him, and give it to him who has ten talents." (v26-28)

'For to everyone who <u>has, more will be given</u>, and he will have abundance; but from him who does not have, even <u>what he has will be taken away</u>. And cast the unprofitable servant into the outer darkness. There will be weeping and gnashing of teeth.' (v29-30)

Here we have a similar parable but with some noticeable differences. A master was about to travel and entrusted his **property** to his servants—**according to their**

abilities. <u>He did not expect more than what they were capable of.</u> Property refers to what he owned. It could have been a number of things apart from his land, such as his possessions, wealth, substance, crops, livestock, etc.

To one he gave five talents (five gold coins), to one two and the third received only one. Now again, a talent on today's currency is over 2 million. The first man went and **traded with it** and gained five more talents (10 million). The second gained two more talents (4 million) while the third dug and hid it in the ground. When the master came to <u>settle accounts</u>, he commended the man who gained five and the man who gained two and said he would make them **ruler over many things.** He told them to enter into the joy of the Lord.

However, the servant who hid the talent in the ground was called a **wicked and lazy servant** and was told he should have, at least, <u>put it into the bank where he could have received some interest on it.</u> Again, it was taken from him and given to the one who had ten talents!

"For to everyone who has, more will be given, and he will have an abundance; but from him who does not have, even what he has will be taken away." (v29)

Some people preach this parable is about our giftings, but to me it is clearly **also** <u>about finances.</u> A talent of gold was part of the currency of the time. 0ur currencies are based on the gold standard value, which fluctuates. The wicked and lazy servant could have put the money in the bank to gain interest. What has that to do with our gifts? Yes, we do need to steward and use our gifts. It is very interesting that he gave them **according to their ability**. God does not expect you to achieve something you are not capable of!

In verse 16 they **traded** – did business to make a gain. The man with five traded and got five more. The man with two traded and got two more. God wants us to be fruitful and have a harvest in our lives, according to our ability. They were called good and faithful servants.

In the Greek, the word used here for servant is '*doulos*', which means slave. That person had no rights as he was bound to his master. It means to do the will of the master to further his kingdom. We are His bondservants in the world with a mandate to extend His Kingdom on earth. He distributes gifts as needed for His Kingdom work. For example, some are called to preaching, some for healing, some for hospitality, some for music and creative things, some for managing finances. We all have different gifts. The point is, we need to grow these gifts and use them for God's Kingdom. What gifts has God given you? Are you growing them and using them for His Kingdom. Are you being faithful?

Section Five - Parables of Mercy and the Love of God

- Parable of the Good Samaritan
- Parable of the Lost Sheep
- Parable of the Lost Coin
- Parable of the Lost Son (also known as the Prodigal Son)
- Parable of the Wicked Vinedressers

Parable of the Good Samaritan (Luke 10:25-37)

There was a young lawyer who came to Jesus asking about eternal life. Jesus replied by asking him what was written in the Law.

> *"So he answered and said,* 'You shall love the LORD your God with all your heart, with all your soul, with all your strength, and with all your mind,' *and* 'your neighbour as yourself.'" (v27)
>
> *And He said to him, "You have answered rightly; do this and you will live."* (v28)

We know that if we look at the Ten Commandments, that the first four are towards God, but the last six are about how we treat others. It is important to see how this relates to this parable which was Jesus' reply to the question of who is our neighbour, or who should we help.

"But he, wanting to justify himself, said to Jesus, "And who is my neighbour?" (v29). So, the parable of the Good Samaritan follows as an example of 'who is my neighbour'!

"Then Jesus answered and said: "A certain man went down from Jerusalem to Jericho, and fell among thieves, who stripped him of his clothing, wounded him, and departed, leaving him half dead. Now by chance a certain priest came down that road. And when he saw him, he passed by on the other side. Likewise, a Levite, when he arrived at the place, came and looked, and passed by on the other side." (v30-32)

"But a certain Samaritan, (a despised foreigner) as he journeyed, came where he was. And when he saw him, he had <u>compassion</u>. So, he went to him and bandaged his wounds, pouring on oil and wine; and he set him on his own animal, brought him to an inn, and took care of him. On the next day, when he departed, he took out two denarii, gave them to the innkeeper, and said to him, 'Take care of him; and whatever more you spend, when I come again, I will repay you.' (v33-35)

"So, which of these three do you think was neighbour to him who fell among the thieves?"
And he said, "He who showed mercy on him."

Then, Jesus said to him, ***"Go and do likewise."*** (v36-37)

This is a parable that demonstrates the love of God for mankind. It also reflects how we are to treat one another. It is hard to explain love, as love is an abstract thing, but by putting it in a story, the meaning becomes clearer to people. The priest (religious leader in charge of the sacrifices), the Levite (musician or singer in the temple) passed by on the other side. They were not willing to help the man. But then a Samaritan, (a foreigner who was despised) saw him and had <u>compassion on him</u> and helped him. Jesus is giving us an example of how we should help others. Remember Jesus said *'do this and you will live'*. We always have a choice to do good or bad.

Right through the Bible ,we see the heart of God to show compassion and look after the poor and those worse off than ourselves. In Leviticus 23:22, they were told not to harvest the edges of their grain fields. If you image a square field and draw a circle in it, then the edges outside the circle were to be left for the poor and the strangers (immigrants) in the land. It was more than a tithe—about twelve and a half percent!

Again, in Deuteronomy, we find the reason for this.

"But you shall remember that you were a slave in Egypt, and the Lord your God redeemed you from

there; therefore, I <u>command</u> you to do this thing. "When you reap your harvest in your field, and forget a sheaf in the field, you shall not go back to get it; it shall be <u>for the stranger, the fatherless, and the widow</u>, that the Lord your God may bless you in all the work of your hands." (Deuteronomy 24:18-19)

The people were to remember that they were slaves in Egypt—the poorest of the poor, so they were to help others who were poor, orphans, widows and strangers in the land, <u>so blessing could come!</u>

In the New Testament we also see the same heart of God reflected. Firstly, in Acts 6, they had a feeding programme for widows. In Galatians, we see how the elders in Jerusalem told Paul they wanted him to look after the poor and also to do good, especially towards believers. It is part of our expression of faith. *"I will show you my faith by my good works"* (James 2:18). This has nothing to do with 'earning our salvation' but follows our salvation so God can bless us as we do what is on His heart. *"They desired only that we should remember the poor, the very thing which I also was eager to do"* (Galatians 2:10).

"Therefore, as we have opportunity, let us do good to all, especially to those who are of the household of faith." (Galatians 6:10)

The Parable of the Lost Sheep (Luke 15:1-7)

Here we have a parable of the shepherd leaving the 99 sheep to go and look for the missing one. When he finds it, he puts it on his shoulders and comes home and calls his neighbours and friends to rejoice with him as he found it. You see God wants all to come to repentance and find His love. So, when someone strays away from the truth, He will leave those that do not need saving to find/help that one soul who is lost.

> *" Jesus answered and said to them, "Those who are well have no need of a physician, but those who are sick. I have not come to call the righteous, but sinners, to repentance."* (James 5:31-32)

The Parable of the Lost Coin (Luke 15:8-10)

A woman lost a silver coin, which would have been valuable. It was part of a *semedi*, a beautiful headdress given to a woman when she was betrothed. It represented her upcoming marriage commitment. She swept the house until she found it. Then she called her neighbours to rejoice with her as she found what was missing. (I have a friend who lost her wedding ring and was afraid to tell her husband. She was in a great panic until she eventually found it – in the kitchen sink! You can imagine how she felt). It is a similar thought to the woman losing a silver coin, which would have been valuable.

In both these parables it concludes with saying "there is more joy in heaven over one sinner who repents" (than 99 who do not need to repent)! We have these two short parables as introduction to the main parable to follow. How can you describe the love of God? How can you describe the compassion of God? Putting it into a parable makes it easier to understand.

The Parable of the Lost Son [Prodigal Son] (Luke 15:11-32)

There was a father who had two sons. He was quite wealthy with many servants. The younger went to his father and demanded his inheritance (a very shameful thing to do), which he took, but wasted with wild, prodigal living. (Even the other brother later accused him of spending it on prostitutes.)

There came a famine in the land and he was in need. He got a job looking after the pigs. The famine was so severe that the pigs were eating better than he was! This finally brought him to his senses and he decided to go home and confess his sins to his father and say *'he is not worthy to be his son'*. He is obviously full of guilt and condemnation at this stage.

There is a Jewish tradition we need to understand about. It is called *Kezezah*. If any son shamed his father and returned home, he would be met at the city gate by the elders of the city. They would break a clay pot to declare he was rejected and cut off from the community. The father was not allowed to be there. Knowing this, it was vital that the father reach his son before he came to the city gate.

> *"And he arose and came to his father. But when he was still a great way off, his father saw him and had compassion, and ran and fell on his neck and kissed him. And the son said to him, 'Father, I have sinned against heaven and in your sight, and am no longer worthy to be called your son.'* (Luke 15: 20-21)

> *"But the father said to his servants, 'Bring out the best robe and put it on him, and put a ring on his hand and sandals on his feet. And bring the fatted calf here and kill it, and let us eat and be merry; for this my son was dead and is alive again; he was lost and is found.' And they began to be merry."* (v22-24)

Just imagine for a moment that this is you. You are full of shame and grief at wasting your father's money. You are fully expecting to be rejected by him and cast out of the house, not only by the father but the whole town. You do not know that every day the father has been watching and expecting you to return home. You cannot imagine he still loves you so much, in spite of what you have done.

He comes running to meet you and hugs and kisses you. Even in that culture, at that time, it was a shameful thing for a man that age to run, as his ankles would be seen. You make your confession but it is like he never heard you. Instead, he commands the best robe to be brought to you, sandals for your feet and a ring for your finger. The robe speaks of sonship restored (not willing that you just be a servant but restored to a son with all its rights and privileges), the sandals mean that you are no longer a slave, and the ring speaks of authority. Not only are you accepted back, not as a slave or hired hand but as **a fully restored son.** This demonstrates the love of God for His children that lose their way in life. When we repent and come back to the Father, there is forgiveness (1John 1:9). The father never stopped loving him, in spite of his son's behaviour. Even when we are at our lowest, if we reach out to Father God and call upon His name, He hears us and accepts us.

> *"Then you will call upon Me and go and pray to Me, and I will listen to you. And you will seek Me and find Me, when you search for Me with all your heart. I will be found by you, says the LORD." (*Jeremiah 29:12-14a)

> *"Call to Me, and I will answer you, and show you*

great and mighty things, which you do not know." (Jeremiah 33:3)

"Hear my cry, O God; attend to my prayer. From the end of the earth I will cry to You, When my heart is overwhelmed; Lead me to the rock that is higher than I." (Psalm 61:1-2)

Back to the parable…

"Now his older son was in the field. And as he came and drew near to the house, he heard music and dancing. So, he called one of the servants and asked what these things meant. And he said to him, 'Your brother has come, and because he has received him safe and sound, your father has killed the fatted calf.' (v25-27)

"But he was angry and would not go in. Therefore, his father came out and pleaded with him. So, he answered and said to his father, 'Lo, these many years I have been serving you; I never transgressed your commandment at any time; and yet you never gave me a young goat, that I might make merry with my friends. But as soon as this son of yours came, who has devoured your livelihood with harlots, you killed the fatted calf for him.' (v28-30)

*"And he said to him, 'Son, you are <u>always with me</u>, and <u>all that I have is yours.</u> It was right that we should make merry and be glad, **for your brother was dead and is alive again, and was lost and is found.**'"* (v31-32)

The older son heard the music and rejoicing. He was jealous of his brother and angry and judgemental about him wasting his father's money. He did not have the grace the father had. He also did not understand <u>the heart of his father</u>, that his brother, once dead and lost, was now alive and found so that was reason to rejoice.

We need to understand that God the Father, does not want anyone to perish, but that ALL might come to repentance and forgiveness.

"The Lord is not slack concerning His promise, as some count slackness, but is longsuffering toward us, not willing that any should perish but that all should come to repentance." (2Peter 3:9)

"All that the Father gives Me will come to Me, and the one who comes to Me I will by no means cast out. For I have come down from heaven, not to do My own will, but the will of Him who sent Me. This is the will of the Father who sent Me, that of all He has given Me I should lose nothing,

but should raise it up at the last day." (John 6:37-39)

God will not reject or cast anyone out who comes humbly, in repentance. Compassion is a very difficult thing to understand. We have our own standards and judgements, but *'God's thoughts are higher than our thoughts, and His ways higher than ours'* (Isaiah 55:8-9). We all need to pray for God's love to fill us so we can be people of compassion and mercy as seen in these two parables.

God is love, so all who follow Him should also walk in love. The apostle John spoke much teaching about love. Let's look at it now.

*"Beloved, let us love one another, for love is of God; and everyone who loves is born of God and knows God. He who does not love does not know God, for God is love. In this the love of God was manifested toward us, that God has sent His only begotten Son into the world, that we might live through Him. In this is love, **not that we loved God, but that He loved us and sent His Son to be the propitiation for our sins.** Beloved, if God so loved us, we also ought to love one another* (1John 4:7-11).

This is seen in the Parables of Good Samaritan, the Unforgiving Servant, as well as the Prodigal Son. We should love others and show mercy, as God first loved us and showed His mercy towards us.

*"No one has seen God at any time. If we love one another, God abides in us, and His love has been perfected in us. By this we know that we abide in Him, and He in us, because He has given us of His Spirit. And we have seen and testify that the Father has sent the Son as Saviour of the world. Whoever confesses that Jesus is the Son of God, God abides in him, and he in God. And we have known and believed the love that God has for us. **God is love**, and he who abides in love abides in God, and God in him."* (1John 4:12-16)

*"Love has been perfected among us in this: that we may have boldness in the day of judgement; because as He is, so are we in this world. There is no fear in love; but <u>perfect love casts out fear</u>, because fear involves torment. But he who fears has not been made <u>perfect in love.</u> We love Him because **He first loved us"*** (v17-19).

"If someone says, "I love God," and hates his brother, he is a liar; for he who does not love his brother whom he has seen, how can he love God whom he has not seen? And this commandment we have from Him: that he who loves God must love his brother also" (v20-21).

None of us have perfect love. Jesus came to show us the love of the Father and demonstrated it by laying down His life for us. We need to pray for God to give us mercy and compassion for others and to increase our love and compassion and even for it to be perfected.

Parable of the Wicked Vinedressers (Luke 20:9-19)

Then He began to tell the people this parable: "A certain man planted a vineyard, leased it to vinedressers, and went into a far country for a long time. Now at vintage-time he sent a servant to the vinedressers, that they might give him some of the fruit of the vineyard. But the vinedressers beat him and sent him away empty-handed. Again he sent another servant; and they beat him also, treated him shamefully, and sent him away empty-handed. And again, he sent a third; and they wounded him also and cast him out" (v9-12).

*"Then the owner of the vineyard said, 'What shall I do? I will send my beloved son. Probably they will respect him when they see him.' But when the vinedressers saw him, they reasoned among themselves, saying, 'This is the heir. Come, let us kill him, that the inheritance may be ours.' So, they cast him out of the vineyard and killed him. Therefore, what will the owner of the vineyard do to them? He will come and **destroy those vinedressers** and give the vineyard to others."* (v13-16)

And when they heard it they said, "Certainly not!" Then He looked at them and said, "What then is this that is written: 'The stone which the builders rejected Has become the chief cornerstone?' (v17)

*"Whoever falls on that stone will be broken; but on whomever it falls, it will grind him to powder." And the chief priests and the scribes that very hour sought to lay hands on Him, but they feared the people—**for they knew He had spoken this parable against them.**"* (v18-19)

In this parable we see how a certain man planted a vineyard from which <u>he expected a harvest</u>. He leased it to vinedressers while he went overseas. At harvest, (vintage) he sent a servant to get some of the produce (grapes and wine). They sent him away empty-handed. He sent another servant and they beat him, treated him shamefully (probably cut off his beard) and sent him away empty handed also. He sent a third and they wounded him and cast him out. Finally, he sent his beloved son who was the heir. They seized him and killed him. Then he asked what the vineyard owner would do to them. The answer being, of course, that they would be destroyed (lose their jobs as the vineyard would be given to someone else).

"O Jerusalem, Jerusalem, the one who kills the prophets and stones those who are sent to her! How often I wanted to gather your children together, as a hen gathers her chicks under her

wings, but you were not willing!" (Matthew 23:37)

This is actually a parable about Jesus Christ, the Beloved Son of God being killed. First, over many years, God sent prophets (servants in this parable) whom they beat, mistreated and many times killed. Many of the prophets were killed in Jerusalem. We see how the chief priests and scribes knew it was a parable against them and sought to kill him (v19).

They did not understand that Jesus, the Beloved son and heir, was the chief cornerstone. In ancient times when they built walls, they drove a post into the ground and put a stone there. It was called the cornerstone. Then they ran a rope in two directions to form a right angle. This was so they could build a straight wall. Jesus said whoever fell on that stone (Him) would be broken and whomever it fell on would be ground to powder (destroyed). This is why they knew He spoke it against them.

Jesus' Preparation of the Disciples for His Death

A number of times Jesus said he had to be mistreated, mocked, spat on and crucified. Jesus prepared His disciples bit by bit, but it was too hard for them to understand.

1. *"From that time (this means on a number of occasions), Jesus began to show to His disciples that **He must go to Jerusalem, and suffer many things from the elders and chief priests and scribes, and be killed, and be raised the third day*** (Matthew 16:21). Here, we are told He must suffer from the religious leaders and be killed. If we go to Luke 9:22 it adds that He must be rejected by the chief priests and scribes (religious leaders).

2. This time He adds that He will be betrayed.

   *"Then they departed from there and passed through Galilee, and He did not want anyone to know it. For He taught His disciples and said to them, "The Son of **Man is being betrayed into the hands of men, and they will kill Him. And after He is killed, He rise the third day**. But they did not understand this saying, and were afraid to ask Him." (*Mark 9:30-32)

3. The third time He predicts His death- specifically by crucifixion. Also, we see the Jewish religious leaders will condemn Him to death and hand Him over to the Romans to be mocked, scourged (whipped) and finally crucified.

*"Now Jesus, going up to Jerusalem, took the twelve disciples aside on the road and said to them, "Behold, we are going up to Jerusalem, and the Son of Man will be betrayed to the chief priests and to the scribes; and they will condemn Him to death, **and deliver Him to the Gentiles to mock and to scourge and to crucify. And the third day He will rise again.**"* (Matthew 20:17-19)

4. Again, it is very specific, that He will be crucified at Passover.

*"Now, it came to pass, when Jesus had finished all these sayings, that He said to His disciples "You know that after two days is the Passover, and the Son of Man **will be delivered up to be crucified.**"* (Matthew 16:1-2)

What was Jesus' Purpose in Coming?

You might ask why was it necessary? It's a very good question. Jesus is called the Son of Man a number of times as **His purpose was to save Mankind.** Do you remember the parable of the shepherd who leaves the 99 to go and find the one lost sheep?

*"For the Son of Man has come to **seek and to save that which was lost.**"* (Luke 19:10)

> *"The Lord is not slack concerning His promise, as some count slackness, but is longsuffering toward us, **not willing that any should perish but that all should come to repentance.**"* (2Peter 3:9)

> *"The next day John saw Jesus coming toward him, and said, "Behold! The Lamb of God who takes away the sin of the world!"* (John 1:29)

He also came to destroy the works of the Enemy. Everything of the curse, abuse, cheating, betrayal, every negative thing you can name, He destroyed it on the Cross.

> *"He who sins is of the devil, for the devil has sinned from the beginning. For this purpose (reason), the Son of God was manifested, that <u>He might destroy the works of the devil."</u>* (1John 3:8)

> *"In this the love of God was manifested toward us, that God has sent His only begotten Son into the world, that we might live through Him. In this is love, not that we loved God, but that He loved us and sent His Son to be the propitiation for our sins."* (1John 4:9-10)

Remember propitiation is the act of satisfying the wrath of God towards evil by the sacrifice of His blood. Thank God for His sacrifice.

Chapter 6
Character (Culture) of the Kingdom

IN THE BOOK OF GALATIANS 5, WE HAVE THE NINE FRUITS of the Holy Spirit. We have the <u>fruit within us</u>, as the Kingdom of God is 'within us'. However, we have to choose to operate from these fruits and not from a performance or striving 'to be good," and so on. As we operate from love, patience, etc., that fruit is manifested. They are not exhaustive but are all godly qualities we need to grow in our lives.

> *"But the fruit of the Spirit is love, joy, peace, longsuffering, kindness, goodness, faithfulness, gentleness, self-control."* (Galatians 5:22-23)

- Love
- Joy
- Peace
- Forbearance (patience)

- Kindness
- Goodness
- Faithfulness
- Gentleness
- Self Control

We must remember that all these qualities and characteristics are part of the nature and character of God. As we get closer to Him, we learn about love, kindness, faithfulness, etc.; as He is all of these things. All these qualities are in us as we become like Him.

> *"And the Lord passed before him and proclaimed, 'The Lord, the Lord God, merciful and gracious, longsuffering, and abounding in goodness and truth keeping mercy for thousands (of generations), forgiving iniquity and transgression and sin.'"* (Exodus 34:6-7)

The first fruit is love. This also includes **compassion**, as everything Jesus did, He did from a heart of compassion. He fed the multitude as they were hungry (Matthew 14:13-21). He healed the leper as He had compassion on him (Mark 1:40-43). He raised the widow's dead boy as He knew he was the one that would look after her in her old age (Luke 7:11-17). He even turned the water into wine, so as not to embarrass the family. In the Middle East, to be able to show hospitality and offer food and drink, especially at a wedding (which lasted a week in those days), was an important and inherent part of the culture (John 2:1-11). He also delivered the demoniac in Mark 5:1-10, because He had compassion on him.

In Colossians 3, We are told to put on many things, but <u>the most important thing is love</u>. Love needs to be the <u>motivation</u> for all we do for God and for the Kingdom. It carries on in v17 to '***be rooted and grounded in love***' so we can know the love of Christ in all its fullness.

> *"Above all these things put on love, which is the bond of perfection."* (Ephesians 3:14)

> *"...that Christ may dwell in your hearts through faith; that you, being <u>rooted and grounded in love</u>, may be able to comprehend with all the saints what is the width and length and depth and height— <u>to know the love of Christ</u> which passes knowledge; that you may be filled with all the fullness of God."* (Ephesians 3:17-19)

Of course, in both the Old Testament and the New Testament we are told to *"Love our neighbour as ourself"* (see Leviticus 19:17-18, Luke 10:25-37). If you look at the Ten Commandments as given in Exodus 20:1-17, we see that the first four are towards God and the next six are towards our fellow man. It is love for our parents that causes us to respect and honour them, it is love for our neighbour that stops us murdering, lying, committing adultery, bearing false witness and lusting after his house, wife or any of his possessions.

When Jesus gave the Parable of the Good Samaritan (Luke 10:29-37), it was to give us an example of what it means to 'love your neighbour as yourself'. Both the priest and the Levite (religious leaders) passed by on the other side ignoring his need. Samaritans were foreigners in Israel and despised. They were not Jews, but in this parable, it was the Samaritan who showed mercy or **compassion** to the man robbed, and left half-naked and almost dead on the road. He picked him up, poured oil on his wounds, bandaged him and took him to the inn. He paid for his stay and offered to give more (if more was needed) on his return. Jesus concluded with the words, "Go and do thou likewise."

We know Jesus, *"filled with the Holy Spirit, went about doing good, and healing all who were oppressed of the Devil"* (Acts 10:38). As we are filled with the Holy Spirit, we can also do 'good works' and manifest the fruit of the Spirit.

Secondly, we have **JOY.** Joy comes from the presence of God.

> *"Therefore, my heart is glad, and my glory rejoices; My flesh also will rest in hope."* (Psalm 16:9)

Pursuing Righteousness

"You will show me the path of life; ***In Your presence is fullness of joy;*** *At Your right hand are pleasures forevermore."* (Psalm 16:11)

We know the joy of the Lord is our Strength. Joy is a noun, but rejoicing is a verb. We are commanded to rejoice. It literally means to return to the source of my joy.

"The Lord is my strength and my shield; My heart trusted in Him, and I am helped; Therefore my heart greatly rejoices, And with my song I will praise Him. The Lord is their strength, And He is the saving refuge of His anointed." (Psalm 28:7-8)

"Do not sorrow, for the joy of the Lord is your strength." (Nehemiah 8:10)

"Rejoice *in the Lord* ***always****. Again, I will say,* ***rejoice!****"* (Philippians 4:4)

So, we are commanded to rejoice – be full of joy – always. We do this by God's joy being in us and overflowing to others. He wants His joy to remain in us.

"These things I have spoken to you, that My joy may remain in you, and that your joy may be full." (John 15:11)

Even when we go through difficulties and trials, we are to count them as joy, because they will give us patience, which will bring us perfection or maturity in the Hebrew.

> *"My brethren, count it all joy when you fall into various trials, knowing that the testing of your faith produces patience. But let patience have its perfect work, that you may be perfect and complete, lacking nothing."* (James 1:2-4)

> *"Now may the God of hope fill you with all **joy and peace** in believing, that you may abound in hope by the power of the Holy Spirit."* (Romans 15:13)

Peace

Peace is the third fruit of the Holy Spirit. If you look at the cover, you will see peace is part of the Cross as pictured from Psalm 85:11. We should *'be in peace'*, *'walk in peace'* and release peace to others, as we have been given peace and the ministry of reconciliation. Christ Himself, gives us His supernatural peace no matter what is happening around us. He IS peace. When we abide in Him, we receive His peace. Also, we are to be in peace with ALL men. That means we must have forgiven those who have treated us wrongly, because you cannot have peace without forgiveness.

"Peace, I leave with you, <u>My peace</u> I give to you; not as the world gives do I give to you. Let not your heart be troubled, neither let it be afraid." (John 14:27)

"These things I have spoken to you, that in Me you may have <u>peace</u>. In the world you will have tribulation; but be of good cheer, I have overcome the world." (John 16:33)

"Now all things are of God, who has reconciled us to Himself through Jesus Christ, and has given us the <u>ministry of reconciliation</u>, that is, that God was in Christ reconciling the world to Himself, not imputing their trespasses to them, and has committed to us the word of reconciliation." (2Corinthians 5:18-19)

"If it is possible, as much as depends on you, live peaceably with all men." (Romans 12:18)

Colossians 3:12-15 tells us of a number of qualities to put on: tender mercies, kindness, humility, meekness, longsuffering; bearing and forgiving one another, love and finally peace.

"Therefore, as the elect of God, holy and beloved, put on tender mercies, kindness, humility, meekness, longsuffering: bearing with

*one another, and forgiving one another, if anyone has a complaint against another; even as Christ forgave you, so you also must do. But above all these things put on love, which is the bond of perfection. And **let the peace of God rule in your hearts,** to which also you were called in one body; and be thankful."* (Colossians 3:12-15)

Next, we come to forbearance or patience.

Forbearance can be described as self-restraint or patience. It implies holding back from what we want to do. We know that "love is patient and kind" (1Corinthians 14:4).

We have already looked at James 1:2-4, where it tells us to count our trials as joy, so patience can work in us to produce maturity.

We are told in Romans 12:12 to be *"joyful in hope, **Patient in affliction**, faithful in prayer."* This has a meaning like standing our ground when in trouble. In other words, we will not 'buckle at the knees,' but stand strong.

> *"Or do you despise the riches of His goodness, **forbearance**, and longsuffering, not knowing that the goodness of God leads you to repentance?"* (Romans 2:4)

God Himself is patient with us, not willing that any should perish but that all should come to repentance. We also then need to develop patience in our lives. I know in this instant generation, we want things to happen immediately, but the best things, like cheese, take time to mature. But, it is through <u>faith and **patience**</u>, that we inherit the promises.

> *"The Lord is not slack concerning His promise, as some count slackness, but is **patient (longsuffering)** toward us, not willing that any should perish but that all should come to repentance."* (2Peter 3:9)

> *"...that you do not become sluggish, but imitate those who through faith and **patience** inherit the promises."* (Hebrews 6:12)

Kindness

We saw how love is patient and **kind**. We also saw in Colossians 3, how we are to 'put on **kindness**'. We are told that *"whoever pursues righteousness and **kindness** will find life, righteousness and honour"* (Proverbs 21:21).

It means to show mercy and compassion to one another, not judging them. Sometimes, this means not saying anything to offend—"biting your tongue." Our words can very quickly 'tear down,' so being slow to speak, and only speaking kind words is important. There is a great principle to live by found in Matthew 7:12, *"do unto others, as you would have them do unto you."*

"And be **kind** to one another, tenderhearted, forgiving one another, even as God in Christ forgave you." (Ephesians 4:32)

Goodness

"Oh, give thanks to the Lord, for He is good! For His mercy endures forever:" (Psalm 107:1)

We know that God is good. His goodness never ceases. The Hebrew word is *chesed*, or lovingkindness. We see this in the Psalms. His lovingkindness is in the morning (Psalm 92:2); is all day long (Psalm 42:8); it preserves us (Psalm 40:11); it lets us shelter under His wings (Psalm 36:7); it is better than life (Psalm 63:3); it is goodness (Psalm 69:16); and it revives us (Psalm 119:159).

Just as we choose to be kind to one another, we also choose to show goodness. We saw this in the parable of the Good Samaritan, who showed mercy to the man beaten up.

Faithfulness (sometimes translated Truth)

God is faithful. He does not change His mind like we do. His promises are true and surely will come to pass. His mercy never ceases! We also read in Exodus 34:6 that *'He is a God of compassion and mercy, slow to anger and abounding in lovingkindness'*.

> *"Through the Lord's mercies we are not consumed, Because His compassions fail not. They are new every morning; Great is Your <u>faithfulness</u>."* (Lamentation 3:2-3)

> *"For I proclaim the name of the Lord: Ascribe greatness to our God. He is the Rock, His work is perfect; For all His ways are justice, A God of truth **(faithfulness**) and without injustice; Righteous and upright is He."* (Deuteronomy 32:3-4)

In the same way that God is faithful, we also need to be faithful. This includes in your marriage, in finances, in keeping your promises, in doing what we have been assigned to do, in our work etc. Luke 16 speaks a lot about this.

"He who is faithful in what is least is faithful also in much; and he who is unjust in what is least is unjust also in much. Therefore, if you have not been faithful in the unrighteous mammon, who will commit to your trust the true riches? And if you have not been faithful in what is another man's, who will give you what is your own? (Luke 16:10-12)

Here it is telling us three things:

- To be faithful in the **little things** as well as the big things. If we can't be faithful in the little things, we won't be faithful in the big things either (see Parable of the Talents).

- Then we have to be **faithful with money** (unrighteous mammon). I remember a man telling me once, when he had a million dollars, he would sow into my ministry. But surely, if he can't sow even $1 now, he will not even when he is a millionaire. We already talked about stewarding money in the parable of the minas and talents (see chapter five).

- Thirdly, we need to be faithful with **what is another's**. That means looking after their property as if it is your own. In ministry, this means serving the man or woman of God you are placed under, and not seeking to take their place or undermine them.

Gentleness

*"Come to Me, all you who labour and are heavy laden, and I will give you rest. Take My yoke upon you and learn from Me, for I am **gentle** and lowly in heart, and you will find rest for your souls. For My yoke is easy and My burden is light."* (Matthew 11:28-30)

Jesus is gentle, so we are also to be gentle with one another, bearing (putting up with) their weaknesses, and forgiving one another and striving to live in peace.

*"...with all lowliness and **gentleness**, with longsuffering, bearing with one another in love, endeavouring to keep the unity of the Spirit in the bond of peace."* (Ephesians 4:2-3)

*"...to speak evil of no one, to be peaceable, **gentle**, showing all humility to all men."* (Titus 3:2)

Self Control

"Whoever has no rule over his own spirit is like a city broken down without walls." (Proverbs 25:28)

Self control is definitely something you have to GROW, like any fruit. It also means learning to bridle your tongue so you speak words of blessing, not words of cursing (James 3:8-10). This requires putting a guard on our tongue because once we utter evil, condemning, judgemental or untrue words, there is no way to take them back.

"But no man can tame the tongue. It is an unruly evil, full of deadly poison. With it we bless our God and Father, and with it we curse men, who have been made in the similitude (image) of God. Out of the same mouth proceed blessing and cursing. My brethren, these things ought not to be so." (James 3:8-10)

It means controlling anger and rage and our emotions. It is not a sin to feel angry, but if you let your anger go into bad words or bad actions then it is sin. This is where controlling your inner self, or inner man comes in. The truth is we have to rule our emotions and not let them get out of control.

Pursuing Righteousness

*"Against such there is no law. And those who are Christ's have crucified the flesh with <u>its passions and desires</u>. If we live in the Spirit, **let us also walk in the Spirit.**"* (Galatians 2:22-25)

This completes our discussion of the nine fruits of the Spirit. There are some other qualities I want to discuss. We will look at the Scripture in 2Peter first. It tells us <u>another way</u> to know we will not be barren or unfruitful. We all have a foundation of faith in our lives as we are saved by grace, through faith in Jesus Christ. We are told to **add seven character traits to our faith:** virtue (moral excellence), knowledge, self-control, perseverance, godliness, brotherly kindness and love. These are like seven pillars that will <u>stop us from stumbling and being barren</u>.

"But also, for this very reason, giving all diligence, add to your faith virtue, to virtue knowledge, to knowledge self-control, to self-control perseverance, to perseverance godliness, to godliness brotherly kindness, and to brotherly kindness love. For if these things are yours and abound, you will be neither barren nor unfruitful in the knowledge of our Lord Jesus Christ." (2Peter 1:5-8)

Let me write it another way:

- Virtue
- Knowledge
- Self-control (see fruit of the Spirit)
- Perseverance (See the Parable of the Persistent Woman, Chapter 5)
- Godliness
- Brotherly kindness
- Love (see fruit of the Spirit)

"Therefore, brethren, be even more diligent to make your call and election sure, for if you do these things, you will never stumble." (2Peter 1:10)

These are not things that can be imparted by the 'laying on of hands'. Rather, they are character traits that need to be developed in our lives. The mark of a man or woman of God is not how many miracles they can perform, or what gifts they function in, but **their character**!

Virtue (moral character and integrity)

Virtue is an old-fashioned word meaning moral integrity, being sexually pure and having pure motives. It means you will be honest with money, it means being loyal and faithful, showing **integrity** in relationships and business and all that we do. It means to be fair and not show favouritism. It means to have no prejudice. It reminds me of Nathaniel. When Jesus saw him, he gave him a wonderful character reference – *'Nathaniel, in whom there is no guile'* [deceit, hidden motives, lies] (John 1:47).

Knowledge

Knowledge is wisdom that is applied practically, and understanding which comes from the fear of the Lord. It does not mean the gathering of information like a quizzer would do, but seeking God's wisdom and applying it in our lives. This is putting the Word into practice!

> *"But be doers of the Word, and not hearers only, deceiving yourselves. For if anyone is a hearer of the Word and not a doer, he is like a man observing his natural face in a mirror; for he observes himself, goes away, and immediately forgets what kind of man he was. But he who looks into the perfect law of liberty and <u>continues in it</u>, and is not a forgetful hearer but a doer of the work, this one <u>will be blessed in what **he does.**</u>"*
> (James 1:22-25)

Self control, which we have already discussed under the fruits of the Spirit (Galatians 5:22).

Perseverance (Longsuffering, Enduring)

It means not giving up when things get difficult. It means having a steady belief in the promises of God in spite of difficulties, discouragement or not good circumstances. But we need to know that the effect of these difficulties, tribulations, disappointments help produce **perseverance and character within us**. (We looked at the parable of the persistent widow in Chapter five, who did not give up until the judge granted her all her rights).

> *"We also glory in tribulations, knowing the tribulation produces <u>perseverance</u>, and perseverance character, and character hope."* (Romans 5:3)

Paul said in 2Corinthians 12:12 to the Corinthians, *"The true signs of an apostle were accomplished among you with **<u>all perseverance</u>**, in signs and wonders and mighty deeds."* Notice that perseverance comes <u>before</u> the signs and wonders and mighty deeds!

> *"Do not grow weary of doing good, for in due season we will reap, if we do not lose heart [give up]."* (Galatians 6:9)

In our instant world, it is so easy to just give up when the task is too big or overwhelming. We need to go to the rock (Jesus Christ), who keeps us steady in the storm (see

Psalm 61:2; Mark 4:35-41). It is an opportunity for your faith to grow!

Another word for perseverance is **endurance or longsuffering**. We grow our character through suffering, as trials are for our spiritual growth. That's why we are told in James 1:2-4 to rejoice in trials as it's for our spiritual good to mature us.

> *"My Brethren, count it all joy when you fall into various trials (temptations, difficulties, persecutions), knowing that the <u>testing of your faith</u> produces <u>patience (endurance, longsuffering</u>). But let patience have its perfect work, that you may be perfect and complete, lacking nothing."*

God is <u>longsuffering</u> with us, not wanting anyone to perish, but that all should come to repentance (2Peter 3:9). In the same way, God wants to develop this character in us, so we do not crumble when trials come [like the seed that fell into the stony ground. It grew but did not endure, as it had no depth of earth to hold it.] (Matthew 13:20-21)

When you go through trials you are laying a foundation, putting a depth into your life that will help you stand strong and not 'buckle at the knees'. This happens if you have no stability.

. . .

Godliness or God-centredness

It means having your priorities based on the Kingdom of God and *'being about His business'* (Luke 2:29). In 1Timothy 3:16, **godliness** is called a 'mystery'. This means something hidden that comes, by revelation. It can be something that was prophesied, like in Isaiah 7:14, a "virgin shall conceive," that seems impossible that was fulfilled in the coming of the Kingdom of God (Luke 1:30-31).

*"And without controversy great is the **mystery of godliness**: God was manifested in the flesh..."* (The Word became flesh and dwelt among us, John 1:14, called the incarnation.)

Justified in the Spirit, (vindicated by Holy Spirit*) by resurrection power, Seen by angels, Christ appeared to many on earth as well as the heavenly realm, Preached among the Gentiles,* (nations) *Believed on in the world, Received up in glory"* [heaven] (1Timothy 3:16).

The spiritual realm is more real than the earthly realm, but many people are unaware of it and how it affects us or shapes us. That's why spiritual things are mysteries that are not easily understood by the natural mind. *"My ways [God's] are higher than your ways, and My thoughts than your thoughts"* (Isaiah 55:8-9).

Brotherly Kindness

We have been commanded to '*Love one another*'. Throughout the Bible is the concept of "Loving your neighbour as yourself" (Leviticus 19:18), which is love from a pure heart. Jesus gave a very good example of loving our neighbour (or fellow man) in the Parable of the Good Samaritan in Luke 10:25-37, which we have already looked at.

Love

The final godly characteristic we need to grow in our life to be fruitful is **love.** Love lasts forever. Love is shed abroad in our hearts by the Holy Spirit. Love is also the most important thing. (Colossians 3:14)

> *"Love suffers long and is kind; love does not envy; love does not parade itself, is not puffed up; does not behave rudely, does not seek its own, is not provoked, thinks no evil; does not rejoice in iniquity, but rejoices in the truth; bears all things, believes all things, hopes all things, endures all things. Love never fails."* (1Corinthians 13:4-8)

Of course, this is the passage given at most wedding ceremonies. However, I would add another passage, which I believe is the best marriage counselling I have ever heard anyone give.

It says to "<u>prefer one another</u>" in love. It is the opposite of selfishness and wanting 'our own way'. That means I will submit my ideas and not want to push my own way. Can you see how this would work in a marriage? Many marriages break up because of the selfishness of one of the partners, but if you give preference to the other person, there is no selfishness! Love does not seek its own (way).

So, I have given you seven pillars to make the foundation of your faith and character strong, so you will not be barren, **but bear fruit.**

Another aspect of godliness is walking a crucified life and walking in the Spirit. This is someone who has chosen to "put off" the works of the flesh (the old man) as mentioned in Colossians 3:5-9 and to put on the new man (Christ with His Godly characteristics).

Other Characteristics

"Therefore, as the elect of God, holy and beloved, put on tender mercies, kindness, humility, meekness, longsuffering; bearing with one another, and forgiving one another, if anyone has a complaint against another; even as Christ forgave you, so you also must do. But above all these things put on love, which is the bond of perfection." (Colossians 3:12-14)

- Tender mercies (merciful).
- Kindness (see the fruit of the Spirit).
- Humility.
- Meekness.
- Longsuffering.
- Bearing with one another (see Brotherly kindness above).
- Forgiving one another (see Brotherly Kindness above and the Parable of the Unforgiving Servant in chapter five).
- Love (see the fruit of the Spirit).

Meekness

In the Sermon on the Mount Jesus said *"the meek will inherit the earth"* (Matthew 5: 5). Meekness means to have a heart attitude that is willing to submit to God's will or to someone. (Not someone who will take control by force). It also means to not be easily provoked.

> *"Who is wise and understanding among you? Let him show by good conduct that his works are done in **the meekness of wisdom**."* (James 3:13)

Here we learn meekness is part of wisdom and is demonstrated by our works. We know Moses was called the meekest man in all the earth, because he put up with all the complaining of the Children of Israel for 40 years and bore all the grief of Miriam and Aaron also.

*"Now the man Moses was very humble **(meek**, gentle, kind, devoid of self-righteousness), <u>more than any man who was on the face of the earth.</u>"* (Numbers 12:3)

Humility

We discussed humility in the parable of the wheat and the tares (see chapter 5). This is the opposite of pride, which we have just read we are to hate. Arrogance, on the other hand, is thinking you are superior or better than someone else. It's to have a higher opinion of yourself than you ought.

"For I say, through the grace given to me, to everyone who is among you, not to think of himself more highly than he ought to think, but to think soberly, as God has dealt to each one a measure of faith." (Romans 12:3)

Humilty is making ourselves lower, which we are commanded to do. It's also about submission to those in authority over us, and even to one another.

"Likewise, you younger people, submit yourselves to your elders. Yes, all of you be submissive to one another, and <u>be clothed with humility</u>, for "God resists the proud, but <u>gives grace to the humble</u>. Therefore, <u>humble yourselves</u> under the mighty

hand of God, that He may exalt you in due time." (1Peter 5:5-6)

Some other qualities: Fear of the Lord, Truth, Justice and Honour, Fear of the Lord.

"Our Father in heaven, Hallowed (feared, reverenced, holy) be Your name." (Matthew 6:9)

Fear of the Lord means reverence, honour, respect. It is the beginning of wisdom and knowledge (Proverbs 1:7; 9:10). It does not mean fear or being afraid, like fear of the dark.

It prolongs days (Proverbs 10:27), keeps us from evil. We need to learn to hate all evil, as that is understanding, as well as to hate pride and arrogance. These are things that God hates, so we also should hate them so we walk in righteousness.

"And to man He said, 'Behold, the fear of the Lord, that is wisdom, And to depart from evil is understanding.'" (Job 28:28)

"The fear of the Lord is to hate evil; Pride and arrogance and the evil way, And the perverse mouth I hate." (Proverbs 8:13)

Not only does the fear of the Lord prolong our days and give understanding, wisdom and knowledge but also gives riches, honour and life.

> *"By **humility** and the **fear of the Lord** Are riches and honour and life."* (Proverbs 22:4)

Truth

***'Jesus full of grace and truth'*. Truth is part of the nature of God.**

"And the Word became flesh and dwelt among us, and we beheld His glory, the glory as of the only begotten of the Father, full of grace and truth." And verses 16-17 *"and of His fullness we have all received, and grace for grace. For the law was given through Moses, but **grace and truth came through Jesus Christ"*** (John 1:14, 16-17)

*"Jesus is the way, **the truth** and the life"* (John 14:6). There is no falsehood, deceit or lying with Father, Son and Holy Spirit. They are called "holy" for a reason!

> *"God is not a man, that He should lie, Nor a son of man, that He should repent. Has He said, and will He not do? Or has He spoken, and will He not make it good?"* (Numbers 23:19)

If God says He will do something, you can rely on Him to do it! In the same way He tells us, *"But let your 'Yes'* *be 'Yes,' and your 'No,' 'No.' For whatever is more than these is from the evil one" (*Matthew 5:37).

We have to learn to develop truth in the 'inward parts' so what comes out of our mouth is truth (see Psalm 51:6-14). This is the prayer of King David after he sinned with Bathsheba. We know that every evil thing is conceived first in the heart, which is why we need to guard our hearts to walk in truth. For out of the heart come evil thoughts (Matthew 15:19).

> *"The heart of the righteous studies how to answer, but the mouth of the wicked pours forth evil."* (Proverbs 15:28)

As far back as the Ten Commandments, we were told *"not to bear false witness against our neighbour"* (Exodus 20:16). This is commandment number nine.

> *"He who **speaks truth declares righteousness**, But a false witness, deceit. There is one who speaks like the piercings of a sword, But the tongue of the wise promotes health. The truthful lip shall be established forever, But a lying tongue is but for a moment. Deceit is in the heart of those who devise evil, But counsellors of peace have joy. No grave trouble will overtake the **righteous,** But the wicked shall be filled with evil. Lying lips are an abomination to the LORD, But*

*those who **deal truthfully** are His delight."* (Proverbs 12:17-22)

Once again, we see the relationship between truth and righteousness. Remember our picture of the Cross on the cover of this book. Righteousness coming down from heaven and truth springing up from the earth (Psalm 85:10-11). The truthful lips will be established forever but lying lips are an abomination to God. If you read Proverbs 6:17, you will see a lying tongue is something that God hates! This is because it is the opposite of truth and the opposite of the nature of God. As Kingdom people we need to learn to walk in truth.

"We are of God. He who knows God hears us; he who is not of God does not hear us. By this we know the spirit of truth and the spirit of error." (1John 4:6)

Clearly there is a Spirit from God called Truth, just as much as there is a false spirit of deception and error that we need to be on guard against, especially in the last days when we know many false spirits will come. There will be false apostles, false prophets, false teachers, false doctrines, false brethren. That is why we are told to "test the spirits" to see if they are from God or not. Do not be naïve. The devil can appear as an angel of light.

Pursuing Righteousness

Many years ago, my pastor woke up to see an 'angel' sitting on his bed. This angel began to tell him to do this and that in the church. After some time, my pastor became uncomfortable and asked the spirit to confess Jesus Christ came in the flesh. This 'angel' turned black and disappeared in a puff of smoke. This is a true story from the 1980's.

Part of the armour of God for every Christian is the '<u>belt of truth</u>' as found in Ephesians 6:14. Paul wrote to Timothy, his son in the faith "to be approved by God, a worker who does not need to be ashamed, who can "<u>correctly handle or divide the word of truth</u>" (2Timothy 2:15).

What does this mean? The Greek word is *orthotomounta*. Ortho means right or proper and tomounta means to cut. This is actually a farming picture of a man who is ploughing. He has to 'cut a furrow', and it has to be straight. So, he focuses on a point where he is going to keep it straight. It means to "cut straight" the Word in truth, with no crookedness (deceit, falsehood, lies, error). It means to discern the truth of a matter and interpret Scriptures in the correct way. It means a diligent and careful approach to understand the entire Bible. It means to focus on the things that are important in our faith and have our eyes fixed on Jesus, the author and finisher of our faith.

Justice

The throne of God is established on justice as well as righteousness. That is why we need to pursue both things in our life. We know God is just and shows 'no partiality' (or 'no respecter of persons', Acts 10:34).

"Righteousness and justice are the foundation of Your throne; Mercy (Steadfast love) and truth go before Your face" (Psalm 89:14). Here we have a picture of another Cross (like the cover) except this time the word justice is used in place of peace. Peace is the word *shalom* which means peace, wellbeing and even freedom and justice. God IS just—totally fair.

"He is the Rock, His work is perfect; For all His ways are justice, A God of truth and without injustice; Righteous and upright is He." (Deuteronomy 32:4)

In Isaiah, there is a prophetic picture of the Messiah (Jesus Christ) the One who will bring justice to the earth.

"Behold! My Servant whom I uphold, My Elect One in whom My soul delights! I have put My Spirit upon Him; He will bring forth justice to the Gentiles. He will not cry out, nor raise His voice, Nor cause His voice to be heard in the street. A bruised reed He will not break, And smoking flax He will not quench; He will bring forth justice for

<u>truth</u>. He will not fail nor be discouraged, Till He has established <u>justice in the earth</u>; And the coastlands shall wait for His law." (Isaiah 42:1-4)

We look forward to the return of Jesus Christ, when He will "*rule the nations with a rod of iron*" (Revelation 2:27) and bring justice to the earth.

Honour

Giving honour to those who have worked hard in the Kingdom is part of Kingdom culture too. You can see this in the Old Testament, also, in regard to older people.

> *"You shall rise before the grey headed and honour the presence of an old man, and fear your God: I am the Lord."* (Leviticus 19:32)

We see how the friends and relatives of Jesus only saw Him as the carpenter's son and gave Him no honour as the Son of God, the Messiah. Their <u>lack of honour</u> and unbelief hindered miracles there!

> "*Is this not the carpenter, the Son of Mary, and brother of James, Joses, Judas, and Simon? And are not His sisters here with us?" So they were offended at Him.*" (Mark 6:3)

*"But Jesus said to them, "A prophet is not **without honour** except in his own country, among his own relatives, and in his own house." Now He could do no mighty work there, except that He laid His hands on a few sick people and healed them. And He marvelled because of their unbelief."* (v 4-6)

"Be kindly affectionate to one another with brotherly love, **in honour giving preference to one another.**" (Romans 12:10)

This is Kingdom culture, to honour others as more important than ourselves. Remember, we are all part of the body and the foot cannot say to the hand *'I have no need of you'*. The truth is, we need each other to fully grow into maturity. This also means we will not criticise and show dishonour to people—we will guard our tongues and actions so we give proper honour and respect, especially to our leaders/fathers and those who have spiritual authority over us.

Chapter 7
Mysteries of the Kingdom

WE HAVE ALREADY LOOKED AT HOW JESUS SPOKE mysteries to the disciples in Parables. We see how Jesus taught the multitudes in the morning and at evening he explained the parables in much more depth when the disciples came and asked him the meaning of each parable. He told them in Matthew 13:11 that, *"It was given to them (the disciples) to know the **mysteries of the kingdom of heaven,** but to them (the multitude) it was not given."*

We all know the *"whodunnit"* murder fiction books, where you have to work out who did the crime, who killed the butler. Every mystery has to be researched to be solved. It's like gold that is hidden waiting to be discovered. Wisdom also is like gold. You have to pursue it.

"If you __seek__ her (wisdom) as silver, And search for her as for hidden treasures; Then you will understand the fear of the Lord, And find the knowledge of God." (Proverbs 2:4-5)

There is a meaning in the parables, where Jesus is asking the disciples to go deeper than just the surface meaning, as every parable has a hidden, spiritual meaning. By digging deeper, you will learn many mysteries.

*"But we speak the wisdom of God in a **mystery**, the **hidden wisdom** which God ordained before the ages for our glory, which none of the rulers of this age knew; for had they known, they would not have crucified the Lord of glory. But as it is written: "Eye has not seen, nor ear heard, Nor have entered into the heart of man The things which God has prepared for those who love Him."* (1Corinthians 2:9)

*"But __God has **revealed them to us** through His Spirit__. For the Spirit searches all things, yes, __the deep things of God__. For what man knows the things of a man except the spirit of the man which is in him? Even so no one knows the things of God except the Spirit of God. Now we have received, not the spirit of the world, but the Spirit who is from God, that we might know the things*

that have been freely given to us by God." (1Corinthians 2:10-12)

Jesus Christ was crucified before the foundation of the world. This was the <u>hidden wisdom of God</u> (1Corinthians 2:7), foreknowing that man would betray Him (See 1Peter 1:20). It was hidden from the Devil and his demons, so they could not interfere with it. God has prepared great and mighty things for us, which we cannot even imagine. These things are revealed to us by His Spirit which abides in us. All things are freely given to us. That is why we need to search, so we can come to know the hidden wisdom and deep things of God.

The Four Levels of Reading In Hebraic Thinking

In Hebrew, Rabbinic teaching, there are four levels of reading:

The Story Level (Peshat)

It is just a surface reading like a story – "a sower went out to sow his seed.…'

The Linking of Two Scriptures Together (Remez)

So as to learn a hidden or allegorical meaning. For example, about faith:

> "Another parable He put forth to them, saying: *"The kingdom of heaven is like a <u>mustard seed</u>,*

which a man took and sowed in his field, which indeed is the least of all the seeds; but when it is grown it is greater than the herbs and becomes a tree, so that the birds of the air come and nest in its branches" (Matthew 13:31-32).

Then you go to Matthew 17:20 and it says:

*"... for assuredly, I say to you, if you have **<u>faith as a mustard seed</u>**, you will say to this mountain, 'Move from here to there,' and it will move; and **nothing will be impossible for you.**"*

First it told us about the mustard seed and how it grows, just like faith must grow. Then it says when we exercise that faith nothing will be impossible.

The Prophetic Level (Drash)

It means to enquire so as to argue. We know everything Jesus did, He did to fulfil the Scriptures about Himself, so there are many examples. One of my favourite Scriptures is from Isaiah 61:1-2:

"The Spirit of the Lord GOD is upon Me, Because the LORD has anointed Me To preach good tidings to the poor; He has sent Me to heal the brokenhearted, To proclaim liberty to the captives, And the opening of the prison to those who are bound; To proclaim the acceptable year

of the LORD, *And the day of vengeance of our God."*

Then we go to Luke 4:18-19 and Acts 10:38 and see its fulfilment:

"how God anointed Jesus of Nazareth with the Holy Spirit and with power, who went about doing good and healing all who were oppressed by the devil, for God was with Him."

The "Hidden" or Sod Level

This is where you have to dig things out. If you like, it is the **mysterious or mystical level** that contains the '*treasures of darkness*'.

"I will give you the <u>treasures of darkness</u> And hidden riches of secret places, That you may know that I, the Lord, Who call you by your name, Am the God of Israel." (Isaiah 45:3)

Much of this <u>level can only come by revelation from the Holy Spirit</u>. You see, in Acts 2, on the day of Pentecost the disciples experienced a new thing. They had never been filled with the Holy Spirit and spoken in tongues before. However, <u>Peter knew, by the Holy Spirit,</u> that this was the fulfilment of the words of the Prophet Joel.

"But Peter, standing up with the eleven, raised his voice and said to them, "Men of Judea and all who dwell in Jerusalem, let this be known to you, and heed my words. For these are not drunk, as you suppose, since it is only the third hour of the day. But this is what was spoken by the prophet Joel: (v14-16)

'And it shall come to pass in the last days, says God, That I will pour out of My Spirit on all flesh; Your sons and your daughters shall prophesy, Your young men shall see visions,

Your old men shall dream dreams. And on My menservants and on My maidservants I will pour out My Spirit in those days; And they shall prophesy." (v17-18)

"The secret things belong to the LORD our God, but those things which are <u>revealed belong to us and to our children forever</u>, that we may do all the words of this law." (Deuteronomy 29:29)

"Oh, the depth of the riches both of the wisdom and knowledge of God! How <u>unsearchable are His judgments</u> and His ways past finding out!" (Romans 11:33)

In the New Testament, Paul talks about mysteries 21 times. In the book of Ephesians alone, there are <u>four</u>

mysteries of the kingdom given. We will have a look at some of these.

The Mystery of His Will

*"... having made known to us **the mystery of His will**, according to His good pleasure which He purposed in Himself, that in the dispensation of the fullness of the times He might gather together in one all things in Christ (unity), both which are in heaven and which are on earth—in Him. In Him also we have obtained an inheritance, being predestined according to the purpose of Him who works all things **according to the counsel of His will**, that we who first trusted in Christ should be to the praise of His glory."* (Ephesians 1:9-12)

"God has now revealed His mysterious will regarding Christ – which is to fulfil His own good plan. And that plan is to bring everything together under the authority of Christ – in heaven and on earth." (New Living Translation)

This translation is easier to understand. God's will is a mystery to most, but it is our inheritance in Christ, as well as the unity He desires to see in His body (Ephesians 4:13). It is to see His Kingdom come on earth.

Jesus taught us to pray *"Your kingdom come, **your will be done on earth as it is in heaven"*** (Matthew 6:10). These are words He abided by until the day He died. In fact, just before the Cross, He prayed asking the Father if the cup (of suffering) could pass from Him but submitted to the Father's will.

> *"And He was withdrawn from them about a stone's throw, and He knelt down and prayed, saying, 'Father, if it is Your will, take this cup away from Me;* **nevertheless, not My will, but Yours, be done.'** (Luke 22:41-42)

In the book of John, we learn more about His will. God wants everyone to know about Him, become His 'children' and to behold His glory.

> *"But as many as received Him, to them He gave* **the right to become children of God**, *to those who believe in His name: who were born, not of blood, nor of the will of the flesh,* **nor of the will of man, <u>but {the will} of God</u>**. *And the Word became flesh and dwelt among us, and we beheld His glory, the glory as of the only begotten of the Father, full of grace and truth."* (John 1-12-14)

We learn in 2Peter 3:9 that God does not want anyone to die in sin, but repent.

*"The Lord is not slack concerning His promise, as some count slackness, but is longsuffering toward us, **not willing that any should perish but that all should come to repentance.**"*

Then again in 1Timothy 2:3-4 again it says that all should repent and come to know Him.

"For this is good and acceptable {will} in the sight of God our Savior, who desires <u>all men to be saved and to come to the knowledge of the truth.</u>"

We know it is also the <u>will of God that we keep our bodies holy</u>, as he is holy. So, we are to flee immorality and sexual uncleanness, because our body is the 'temple of the Holy Spirit" (1Corinthians 6:18-20; 1Thessalonians 4:3).

*"For **this is the will of God, your sanctification**: that you should abstain from sexual immorality; that each of you should know how to possess his own vessel in sanctification and honour, not in passion of lust, like the Gentiles who do not know God;* (1Thessalonians 4:3-5).

If we go to Ephesians 5:17-21 We learn more about the will of God.

*"Therefore, do not be unwise, but **understand what the will of the Lord is**. And do not be drunk with wine, in which is dissipation; but <u>be filled with the Spirit</u>, speaking to one another in psalms*

and hymns and spiritual songs, singing and making melody in your heart to the Lord, <u>giving thanks always</u> for all things to God the Father in the name of our Lord Jesus Christ, <u>submitting to one another</u> in the fear of God."

Three things:

1. Be filled with the Holy Spirit outworked in worship.
2. Giving thanks to God in everything (see Philippians 4:6; 1Thessalonians 5:18).
3. Submitting to one another (and preferring one another. (Romans 12:10)

How important is it to do the will of God?

There are always consequences for everything we do outside the will of God. When we do the will of God, we are protected from the evil one. That is part of the prayer the Lord taught us in Matthew 6:10,13. I also want to discuss a passage many people are afraid of and don't understand the context.

> *"Not everyone who says to Me, 'Lord, Lord,' shall enter the kingdom of heaven, **but he who does the will of My Father in heaven.** Many will say to Me in that day, 'Lord, Lord, have we not prophesied in Your name, cast out demons in Your*

*name, and done many wonders in Your name?' And then I will declare to them, 'I never knew you; depart from Me, you who practice **lawlessness!'*** (Matthew 7:21-23)

Those who do not do the will of God are those who do lawlessness – without righteousness, without keeping the ways of God. Clearly seeking to do the will of God is VERY important.

The Mystery of the Gospel/Salvation

When we read Ephesians 3:1-5, we see that Gentiles have become fellow heirs and members of the same body.

*"...how that by revelation He made known to me **the mystery** (as I have briefly written already, by which, when you read, you may understand **my knowledge in the mystery of Christ**), which in other ages was not made known to the sons of men, as it has now been revealed by the Spirit <u>to His holy apostles and prophets.</u>"* (Ephesians 3:3-5)

*"Now to Him who is able to establish you according to my gospel and the preaching of Jesus Christ, according to the **revelation of the mystery kept secret since the world began,** but now made manifest, and by the prophetic Scriptures made known to all nations,*

according to the commandment of the everlasting God, for obedience to the faith." (Romans 16:25-26)

<u>What is this mystery</u>? It is that Jesus Christ was crucified before the foundation of the world and that our sins can be forgiven as we believe in Him, by faith.

> *"but, with the precious blood of Christ, as of a lamb without blemish and without spot. He indeed was <u>foreordained before the foundation of the world</u>, but was manifest in these last times for you, who through Him believe in God, who raised Him from the dead and gave Him glory, so that your faith and hope are in God."* (1Peter 1:19-21)

God's plan was to send His only begotten Son into the world to be crucified, so His blood could atone (pay for) for our sins. The promise was to anyone who would believe in Him. He would satisfy the wrath of God towards sin by becoming the *'propitiation for our sin'* (1 John 2:2).

> *"For God so loved the world that He gave His only begotten Son, that whoever believes in Him should not perish but have everlasting life. For God did not send His Son into the world to condemn the world, <u>but that the world through Him might be saved.</u>"* (John 3:16-17)

Inclusion of the Gentiles in the Plan of Salvation

We see that Gentiles have become fellow heirs and members of the same body of Christ.

> *"that the Gentiles should be <u>fellow heirs, of the same body</u>, and partakers of His promise in Christ through the Gospel, of which I became a minister, according to the gift of the grace of God given to me, by the effective working of His power."* (Ephesians 3:5-7)

We have already seen how Jesus was crucified before the foundation of the world but this 'mystery' was hidden from the ruling powers, or He would not have been crucified! It was part of God's plan of salvation for **all people** to come to know Him and be forgiven of their sins. Then it carries on, not only the Jews, **but also the Gentiles** (that's us, unless you are Jewish), were to be included in His body. Let us read the whole passage.

> *"For this reason I, Paul, the prisoner of Christ Jesus <u>for you Gentiles</u>— if indeed you have heard of the dispensation of the grace of God which was given to me for you, how that by revelation He made known to me **the mystery** (as I have briefly written already, by which, when you read, you may understand my **knowledge in the mystery of Christ**), which in other ages was not made known*

to the sons of men, as it has now <u>*been revealed by the Spirit to His holy apostles and prophets*</u>*:* ***that the Gentiles should be fellow heirs,*** *of the same body, and partakers of His promise in Christ through the gospel, of which I became a minister according to the gift of the grace of God given to me by the effective working of His power."* (Ephesians 3:1-7)

"For you are all sons of God through faith in Christ Jesus. For all of you who were baptized into Christ have clothed yourselves with Christ. There is neither Jew nor Greek, there is neither slave nor free man, there is neither male nor female; for you are all one in Christ Jesus." (Galatians 3:26-28)

"For He Himself is our peace, who made both groups into one and broke down the barrier of the dividing wall, by abolishing in His flesh the enmity, which is the Law of commandments contained in ordinances, so that in Himself He might make the two into one new man, thus establishing peace..." (Ephesians 2:14-15)

Through Christ we are one new man. There is no division between Jew and Gentile (or any other nation, or gender or nationality division either). That middle wall of separation has been broken through the Cross (His flesh), to bring in a New Covenant.

Let's look at the call of God to Saul (later named Paul) and his encounter on the way to Damascus. It is a very specific call—to open their eyes, to bring them out of darkness and Satan's power, that they can be forgiven and receive an inheritance! It was a specific call to the Gentiles. (Peter was called to the Jews.)

> *"Rise and stand on your feet; for I have appeared to you for this purpose, to make you a minister and a witness both of the things which you have seen and of the things which <u>I will yet reveal to you</u>. I will deliver you from the Jewish people, **as well as from the Gentiles, to whom I now send you,** to open their eyes, in order to turn them from darkness to light, and from the power of Satan to God, that they may receive forgiveness of sins and an inheritance among those who are sanctified by faith in Me.'* (Acts 26:16-18)

*"The **mystery** which has been hidden from ages and from generations, but now has been revealed to His saints. To them (the saints), God willed to make known what are the riches of the glory of this **mystery among the Gentiles**: which is **<u>Christ in you, the hope of glory.</u>**"* (Colossians 1:27)

So, the mystery is contained <u>within us</u>. We have the Kingdom within us (Luke 17:21). Therefore, we can know what was hidden for generations as it is now made known to us— the riches of His glory, our inheritance and hope of glory (hope of the resurrection).

If we study the genealogy of Jesus, we also see <u>the inclusion of Gentiles in the Plan of Salvation</u>. The Mother of Boaz was Rahab from Jericho, and Obed's Mother was Ruth, a Moabitess (Luke 3:23-38).

The Mystery of His Fellowship

*"To me, who am less than the least of all the saints, this grace was given, that I should preach among the Gentiles the unsearchable riches of Christ, and to make all see **what the fellowship is of the mystery, which from the beginning of the ages has been hidden in God who created all things through Jesus Christ;** to the intent that now the manifold wisdom of God might be made known by the church to the principalities and powers in the heavenly places, according to the <u>eternal purpose which He accomplished in Christ Jesus our Lord,</u> in whom we have boldness and access with confidence through faith in Him."* (Ephesians 3:8-12)

"and raised us up together, and made us sit together in the heavenly places in Christ Jesus." (Ephesians 2:6)

We know when Jesus died, the curtain of the temple was torn in two, from top to bottom, literally making a way into the Holy of Holies (Matthew 27:51). Only the high priest was allowed to enter there, once a year on the Day of Atonement (Yom Kippur), to sprinkle the blood on the mercy seat for the sins of the nation. Now, because of His death and resurrection, we can *'come boldly to the throne of Grace to receive mercy and grace'* (Hebrews 4:16). His own blood was shed, **once and for all**, to cleanse our consciences from dead works (religion, doing things in our own strength and what is right in our own eyes). (See Hebrews 9:12-14.)

The Mystery is of the Relationship of a Man and a Woman

In Genesis 2, we see that there was no helper or helpmate for Adam. There was no one comparable to him. This has the meaning of 'fitting like a glove'.

"But for Adam there was not found a helper comparable to him (verse 20).

> *"And the LORD God caused a deep sleep to fall on Adam, and he slept; and He took one of his ribs,*

and closed up the flesh in its place. Then the rib which the LORD God had taken from man He made into a woman, and He brought her to the man." (v 21-22)

And Adam said: <u>'This is now bone of my bones And flesh of my flesh; She shall be called Woman'</u>, Therefore, a man shall leave his father and mother and be joined to his wife, and they shall become one flesh. And they were both naked, the man and his wife, and were not ashamed." (v23-25)

When we understand the Hebrew word comparable *(kenegedo)*, we see the Divine plan of God for a man and a woman in marriage. God made mankind from the dust of the earth and breathed into his nostrils so he became a living being. Then He took a rib from Adam's side and formed a woman and brought her to the man. She was designed <u>to be comparable to him</u>. We say a soulmate, or helpmate. The word literally means *'against'*. God has placed wisdom in the woman to be *'against him'* if he follows the wrong path. I have seen this many times when God gives a dream or impression to the wife to stop her husband from making the wrong choice.

We read in Ephesians 5:25-28; 31-32 this mystery is about Christ and the church (His bride).

"Husbands, love your wives, just as Christ also loved the church and gave Himself for her, that He might sanctify and cleanse her with the washing of water by the word, that He might present her to Himself a glorious church, not having spot or wrinkle or any such thing, but that she should be holy and without blemish. So, husbands ought to love their own wives as their own bodies; he who loves his wife loves himself." (v25-28)

*"For this reason, a man shall leave his father and mother and be joined to his wife, and the two shall become one flesh." This is a great **mystery**, but I speak concerning Christ and the church."* (v31-32)

In the book of Proverbs, it speaks about three things too wonderful -an eagle in the air, a serpent on a rock, a ship on the sea. Then it says there is a fourth thing, which I don't understand – a man with a virgin (Proverbs 30:18-19).

In Ephesians, Apostle Paul uses the same picture of Christ and the church. He further states that women should submit to and respect their husbands as Christ loves His church. The church submits to Christ in the same way a wife submits to her husband.

"Wives, submit to <u>your own husbands</u>, as to the Lord. For the husband is head of the wife, as also Christ is head of the church; and He is the Saviour of the body. Therefore, just as the church is subject to Christ, so, let the wives be to <u>their own husbands</u> in everything" (v22-24), and v33 *"Nevertheless let each one of you in particular so love his own wife as himself, and let the wife see that she <u>respects her husband</u>."*

We have already seen in the book of Romans, that we are to "have honour, *preferring one another in love"* (Romans 12:10).

Here it implies submitting to one another as it says in Ephesians 5:21 *"Submit to one another out of reverence for Christ."*

So, we, as the Bride of Christ submit to Him, in the same way a wife submits to her husband and in the same way we are expected to submit to one another. This means I am not superior to you. You have value and I also have value. We can learn from each other.

The Mystery of Godliness

> *"And without controversy, great is the **mystery of godliness**. God was manifested in the flesh, Justified in the Spirit, Seen by angels, Preached among the Gentiles, Believed on in the world, Received up in glory."* (1Timothy 3:16)

Conclusion

It was a mystery that God would make a way for us to know His will and plan for the world. That a virgin would conceive, and that Child would be the Saviour of the world. That He would come that all men might repent and be forgiven, reconciled, justified (made right with God). It was a mystery that not only would the Gospel (Good News) be made known, but that even we, as Gentiles, would be included! Such is the grace of God.

It is a mystery that it was concealed from the principalities and powers, or they would not have crucified the Lord. It is a mystery that God sent His Holy Spirit to come and abide within us and teach us all things, and reveal these mysteries to us. It is a mystery that we have a heavenly inheritance and the **Kingdom of God is within us**, with all the riches of His glory.

Conclusion

There are other mysteries in the Word, more treasures of darkness, but that is for you to research.

About the Author

Sandra Roberts is an ordained pastor who was called of God to go to the nations at age 12. She first went to Korea, then Japan at age 20 with Youth with a Mission (YWAM). She has over thirty years of ministry experience and has a Diploma in Theological Studies (Zion Bible College).

Sandra has been going to the nations since 2009, firstly to South East Asia (Malaysia, Indonesia, Cambodia, Thailand, Sri Lanka, Singapore), Australia, then to India, Pakistan (where she has spent much of her time), the USA, Colombia, Spain, Britain, Kenya, Uganda, Tanzania, Burundi, South Africa and Mauritius. Her ministry is in healing and deliverance, preaching and teaching the Word of God. Sandra functions in all the five- fold ministry anointings. She also ministers on *Shalom Divine TV* in India weekly as well as other platforms.

In 2015, Sandra, along with Pastor Edwin Nazir, planted Breakthrough Church, Breakthrough School and Breakthrough Ministries in Pattoki, Pakistan. Since then, the ministry has grown to ten churches, two schools and a Bible College. She is also actively working in both Uganda and Tanzania with orphans and church planting, evangelism and also in training conferences.

www.ingramcontent.com/pod-product-compliance
Lightning Source LLC
Chambersburg PA
CBHW060532100426
42743CB00009B/1501